..........................Have We
REALLY

Come
A Long
Way?

Bethany House Books by Ruth Senter

••••••••••••••••••••

Can I Afford Time for Friendships?
(with Stormie Omartian & Colleen Evans)

Have We Really Come a Long Way?

Longing for Love

9612

Ruth Senter

..................Have We
REALLY
Come
A Long
Way?

BETHANY HOUSE PUBLISHERS
MINNEAPOLIS, MINNESOTA 55438

Published by Bethany House Publishers
A Ministry of Bethany Fellowship, Inc.
11300 Hampshire Avenue South
Minneapolis, Minnesota 55438

Printed in the United States of America.

Library of Congress Cataloging-in-Publication Data

Senter, Ruth Hollinger
    Have we really come a long way? / Ruth Senter.
       p. cm.
    ISBN 1–55661–820–4
    1. Women—Religious life. 2. Women—United States. 3. Senter,
Ruth Hollinger, 1944–   . I. Title.
BV4527.S355   1997
261.8'344'0973—dc21

                                    96–45870
                                       CIP

RUTH SENTER is the author of nine books. The former editor of *Partnership* magazine and contributing editor to several Christian periodicals, she is also an active speaker. Ruth has a B.A. in communications from the Univerisity of Illinois and an M.A. in journalism from the Wheaton Graduate School. She and her husband, Mark, live in the Chicago area and are the parents of two grown children.

92647

CONTENTS

Introduction 9

1. Have We Really Gotten What We Want?
   Contentment 13

2. What Do We Do With the Past?
   Forgiveness 31

3. Waning Signs of Sisterhood
   Unity 47

4. The Serious Business of Being a Woman
   Humor 65

5. Real Women Don't Cry
   Emotional Sensitivities 81

6. Hiking Solo Up the Mountain
   Our Need for Each Other 97

7. Hang Up the Dreamin'
   The Ability to Reflect 113

8. The Slippery Slope of Women's Rights
   Willingness to Surrender 133

9. Empty on the Inside?
   Spiritual Discipline 149

10. Where Has Tomorrow Gone?
    Hope 165

INTRODUCTION

I'll admit, as a woman of the '90s I enjoy great freedom. I have two academic degrees. I have a career. I serve on the board of an international agency. I sometimes teach both men and women. On top of all that, my husband sometimes fixes dinner. So who am I to say, "I have lost some things to the new day that has dawned for women"?

But I say it, because I have.

Yes, I've gained much. And for that I am truly grateful. I will never forget that it has been easier for me to follow my dream than it was for my mother to follow hers. Nor will I decry the winds of change that have given me wings and offered me the choice to sift through the rubric, claim the helpful (godly, wise, expedient), and toss the rest.

Thank goodness I've had the choice.

But now, looking back on some thirty years of "the new day that has dawned for women," I sense there have been not only dawnings, there have been sunsets too. Some things have disappeared—like the sun over the rim of the earth.

I am sad about the sunsets—the losses, the disappearance of qualities of living that made our mothers and grandmothers strong.

I lament their absence. I pray for their return. And I also light my candle in search of what it is we as women may be giving up that we desperately need to keep. (This is what this book is all about.) And I hope against hope that some candles burning brightly might crack a new dawn—that the sun will rise for women, over equal opportunities, yes, but more importantly, over healthy emotions, whole families, healed relationships, and Christlike qualities of life.

To this end I offer up these thoughts. To this end I share stories of my mother, my grandmothers, and other courageous women who have managed to hang on to what is important. Life varies its stories. Time changes everything, yet what is truly valuable—what is worth keeping—is beyond time. Your story will be different than mine. From a human perspective, some stories seem mostly happy, some mostly sad. But from all, happy or sad, there are lessons to be learned.

So read this book, think about the stories, and then look beyond them to your own story. Find examples there. Learn from the examples—learn what to keep and what to throw away. Learn how the past has shaped you and how the present, threatening though it may be at times, can ultimately lead you to wise, responsible, and godly living.

Have we really come a long way?

That all depends.

Come join me, then, in the exploration.

ONE

....

Sometimes the closer you get to your goal, the more discontent you are with your past and your present. I believe this is where many women are today.

....

Have We Really Gotten What We Want?

Contentment

Today should be a day of great jubilation for women. We have not arrived by any means. But with all our accomplishments and advances, I'd think we would be celebrating that we are so well on our way, that we have come so far.

I'd think we would know some new measure of contentment, of satisfaction that we've achieved so many of our goals.

But contentment is not what I see and hear and feel among women today. I feel the constant yearning, the restless longing, the deepening discontent—as though we have made it over the mountain but can't quite bring ourselves to settle in and call the place home. There is always another ridge we are wanting to cross. Always another peak to conquer. Always voices beckoning us on. *Not quite enough. You haven't gained enough. There's more. There's more.*

What does it all mean, this dissatisfaction over how far we *haven't* come? This always longing for more?

Maybe our freedom has become our ball and chain. Maybe the more we gain, the more gains we want. Maybe we've gotten what we want, but somewhere along the way lost some of the priceless commodities we had.

How have we arrived at this unhappy state of affairs—we, who have made so much progress in so short a time?

Maybe this.

We've long been discontented with the system. We've crusaded long and hard to fix the flaws in it. And yes, much about the system's treatment of women has needed fixing—and in some cases still does. But it seems our dissatisfaction with the system has taken our discontent to a much more personal level, a level deep within ourselves. We've been unhappy with the system for a long time. Now we're unhappy with ourselves and the people around us.

True, some dissatisfaction is necessary. No discontent, no change. Women did not come to this place where we are more free to use our spiritual gifts to service the body of Christ by accepting a church hierarchy that had to hold a council to debate whether women had souls or not. Susan B. Anthony and others did not win us the right to vote by being content with a system that said women were not smart enough to elect their own leaders. Discontentment over these kinds of women's issues was, and continues to be, necessary.

But today it seems our discontent has so seeped into our spirits that we aren't satisfied with much of anything anymore. We are the restless wind, always flitting, never at home.

It has been a subtle shift—this edging toward discontent. I see it not only in our restlessness but also in our inability to enjoy ourselves. Whatever we are doing, we wish we were doing something else. However beautiful or talented we are, we wish we were someone else. We live with such longing.

My great-grandma lived to be ninety-nine years old. Up until several years before she died, she was still climbing a ladder and planting her garden. I cannot say Grandma Diffenbach lived without longing. But she did live with contentment. How do I know? It was written all over her face.

Not that she really had all that much to be content about. Life on the farm was hard. She had lost two daughters before they saw their thirtieth birthdays, and five motherless grandchildren were part of her concern. Her skin was weathered by the years, her hands gnarled with work. But her eyes sparkled to her dying day.

Sometimes I get to wondering: what will I look like if I live as long as Grandma Diffenbach? Will my eyes sparkle? Will my great-grandchildren sense my peace? Will I leave behind a legacy of contentment?

———

I have just returned from visiting my parents. My mother is seventy-nine, and she and my dad live in a two-bedroom ranch home on a quiet, tree-lined street that dead-ends six houses down. Every morning my mother walks up and down that short street to keep the blood flowing freely through her main artery, which was once 97 percent blocked.

My mother has given birth to five children. She has, in her younger years, served with my father as a pioneer missionary in rural Alabama. In her mid-life she finished raising her children, taught Bible clubs, traveled to foreign countries on mission work projects, ministered to women's groups; to name just a few of her pursuits.

Today, in her "retirement," she is out and about most every day with my dad, who is the visitation pastor for a moderately sized church in the East. Together they visit hospitals, nursing homes, retirement centers, prisons—anywhere a needy parishioner happens to be. Even as her eighty-year mark presses in close up on her, hardly a week goes by that she does not invite someone to dinner. It is her way of retiring.

Her industry amazes me. (And makes me tired!) But one thing amazes me more: My mother is the most contented person I know.

———

"What do you want for Christmas?" I ask. It's October and I'm already into a semi-panic about my shopping list.

"I don't know," she answers simply. "I have everything I need."

I am not so easily put off.

"Come on, Mother. You must need *something*."

She is immoveable.

"No. I really don't."

And she actually means it. As far as she is concerned, she has all she needs.

I look around her house. She could use new carpet in the room she and Daddy affectionately refer to as "The Study." It is their private sanctuary—barely big enough for their two recliners, Daddy's big oak desk (which has been around since before time began), a small two-drawer file painted light green to match the walls, and a bookshelf creatively housed in a closet with the doors removed so it looks like part of the room.

The room is appropriately dubbed "The Study" because it's where Daddy studies and prepares his sermons and where he and Mother study their Bible every morning without fail.

The Study is also the platform from which they study the birds, the clouds, the trees. They've set their recliners so they can keep an eye on the world beyond the plate-glass patio doors.

From The Study they examine the world at large. Every evening after the day's news has been digested they fold the newspaper and slip it into the old magazine rack between their two recliners. The newspapers are carried out to the re-cycle bin once a week. But until then, their "textbooks" to the world are kept close at hand. You never know what infor-mation you may need in the course of the week.

"Yes," says Mother. "I have all I need."

But still, The Study does need new carpet, and for all the entertaining Mother's done, she's never had a soup tureen or ice cream dishes or silver napkin rings.

I tell Mother if she can't think of anything she needs, I will think of something for her. And she is just as happy about that. She pulls out her big cast-iron skillet and begins to brown the chicken for dinner. She has no further comment about her needs.

In fact, for as long as I can remember she has not com-mented about her needs. She simply lives from sunup to sun-down, savoring the beauty of the day outside. And if it is rain-ing, she turns on all the lamps in the house and savors the warmth of her cozy rooms. In between the savoring, she tells me how good God is, how fortunate she is to be married to

Daddy, and how wonderful her children are. (No wonder I like to go home.)

True, my mother has her down times just like everyone else. She has walked through many a valley. But I have seen contentment so spelled out in the life of my mother that I could not create the quality in a character more completely were I writing fiction. I get the feeling Mother is content with what she has in the way of material possessions. But there is something even deeper. I sense she is content with who she is and what she does.

Being with my mother always arouses a certain sad nostalgia. I am not wishing back my childhood, as warm and nurturing as it was. But I *am* wishing back the contentment I find in my mother. I wish it for myself. I wish it for women everywhere who seem so restless, so filled with longing.

Sometimes I wonder about this old-fashioned brand of serenity I saw in my great-grandma and see today in my mother. I cannot say for sure exactly what it was. Certainly, it had to do with their walk with God. With their strength of character. But I suspect it also had something to do with their belief that they were significant.

Perhaps the discontent among women today has something to do with our feelings of insignificance. Perhaps we are not so sure where our significance comes from anymore.

———

Time was, women seemed to believe they were significant no matter what they did. Today, it all depends on how we spend our days, what our annual salary is, and whether we have a title or degree after our name.

I once thought I was significant simply because I belonged to God—had been bought by him for an enormous price. And

I did not need to prove myself worthy of that price tag. Back then, it was enough for me to honor God, love my husband, raise my children, enjoy birdsong, plant a garden, clean out the garage, write a song or a sonnet or whatever it was inside me at the time that needed to come out.

I honored God because I belonged to him. I loved my husband because I committed myself to love him. I raised my children because I brought them into the world. I cleaned my garage because it got dirty. I listened to birdsong because my mother saw to it that my ear was trained. I planted a garden because I love the feel of dirt under my fingernails. I wrote a song, sonnet or whatever because I could not help but do it.

But then, along came someone and said that wasn't enough—I needed to prove my significance by *doing* something more. I can't name the person who told me. No one ever looked me in the eye and blurted it out. Or wrote me a letter or called me on the phone to break the news. But I heard it from collective voices who subtly dropped the hint: Whatever you're doing, it's outdated. There's a whole new world waiting for you out there. And you'll never find it cleaning out your garage.

Granted, I did not earn my academic degrees cleaning out my garage. Nor did digging around in my garden land me any book contracts. But who's to say it was not enough? Who's to say I was not just as significant whether I was studying Festinger's Cognitive Dissonance for my Master's degree or planting Dutch tulips in my backyard?

Used to be, I decided for myself where my significance came from. I got my clues from God. But now other voices are trying to help me decide. And the impression I get is this: significant things for women can only happen in boardrooms, classrooms, courtrooms, newsrooms, or some such place.

The irony is that some of the moments of my life when I've most sensed that what I'm doing may actually be leaving a legacy for eternity have occurred in my children's bedrooms or in our family room or around our kitchen table. Those have been the times I've looked into the faces of the ones I love and said to myself, "I am helping them become all they can be. Life doesn't get much better than this."

But that was before the rumbling that *that* wasn't enough.

Seems to me, there's something wrong with that rumble. It is based on the faulty assumption that significance is something I do for myself. Wrong. My significance has nothing to do with me. It has everything to do with God. He made me. Stamped me with his image. Loved me enough to exchange places with me. (He went to the cross. I went free.) That's significance.

Unfortunately, we spend our lives trying to prove our significance. And even more unfortunately, we depend on shallow criteria for proof—criteria such as whether we work inside the four walls of our home or outside them.

Whether a woman works outside the home or not is a matter of economics and calling. Whether she has a title, a staff, a degree—that is a matter of opportunity. But such things are NOT matters of significance. Carrying a briefcase to an office did not make me significant. Neither did staying home and playing *Missing Matchups* with our two preschoolers. (Nor did one make me more spiritual than the other.)

The core of my significance is this: I am God's. Made for him. Made like him. Made to be his forever. I draw my significance and value from God's likeness in me, not from what the multiple voices are telling me that I, as a Christian woman, should be doing with my days. Significance has nothing to do with my profession and everything to do with my confession:

"Lord, your stamp of approval is upon me."

What does all this have to do with contentment?

Simply this: If God (not the "multiple voices") is my "shepherd" *then* "I shall not want" (Psalm 23:1, KJV). I can graze contentedly in the green pastures rather than always wanting to jump the fence for the greener pastures beyond.

"The Lord is my shepherd; I shall not want."

Oh, but we DO want. We want what we don't have. We want what we can't have.

Take marriage, for example.

If divorce statistics tell us anything, they tell us this: There was a time when women were more content with their husbands. Or, if you weren't completely satisfied with him, at least you stuck with him. Back then, husbands were not so easily swapped, traded, or discarded.

But times have changed.

———

I talked to my mother last night on the phone. Last night was Halloween, so I waited till later to call. I knew she would be giving out apples and peanut butter candy to the children in her neighborhood.

"Just tucked Daddy into bed and rubbed his back and legs with Aspercreme," she said. "He had five hospital calls today . . . and with all the rain, he's feeling the aches tonight."

Daddy has had four back operations and walks with a cane. When he performs weddings, he uses a pulpit so he has something to lean against. Last time I was home, I noticed he was reaching out for the walls more often when he walked around the house.

But every night before he goes to bed, he and Mother play a game of *Scrabble* or *Rummykub*. They light candles at dinner, read books out loud to each other, and listen to hymns of praise on the local Christian radio station. Every now and then, they slip away for a day or two at an old inn or a bed-and-breakfast somewhere up in the foothills.

For fifty-six years, my mother has gladly shared her energy with my dad. She cooks his favorite meal—ham loaf and noodles (with saffron), sees to it that his suit is pressed every Saturday night for the Sunday services, and has said to me for as long as I can remember, "Isn't he a dear dad?"

I picture my mother and dad holding hands across their recliners every morning when they have their prayer time together. And I feel the loss. Not for them, but for women everywhere who aren't content with their husbands anymore, who think it is old-fashioned to share your energy with a man.

Seems today, since we have to be more of whatever it is we are, we no longer have energy to spare or share. We need every ounce of what we have for ourselves. Takes much more these days to keep us women running. So whatever crumbs our husbands can gather from beneath our tables will have to do.

Sign the contract here . . . for as long as *my* needs are being met.

Whatever happened to the notion that marriage is a joint union of shared energy, shared surrendering up for the sake of another? Marriage is neither contract nor formula. (One is as deadly as the other.) Marriage is a coming together in a joyful union of mutual surrender.

True, times are more precarious now for women and men. We are together more often in the workplace. In fact, we may spend far more time with another man in an office than we do with our husband at home. Today, men are our colleagues, partners, mentors, associates.

In many ways, the workplace has become the breeding ground for all sorts of discontent. We have more chance to compare, to notice what other men are that our husbands are not. (We forget, men get dressed up to come to work; husbands do not often get dressed up for us at home.)

So how do we survive the man in the gray suit, immaculate white shirt, and silk Dior tie who smiles at us across the desk?

Contentment may not be all there is to the answer, but certainly it is a major part of the answer. Male associations are more likely to be safe territory for us if we are content with our own husband. The minute I begin to feel my husband is not enough for me, I set myself up for inappropriate involvement with someone else.

When we lose contentment, we stand to lose everything. Even our marriages.

———

We may be witnessing a new brand of discontentment today, but women's discontent is not new. The voices of "not enough" have been upsetting our equilibrium ever since the Garden of Eden. In the beginning, God created the heavens and the earth. Yes. But in the beginning he also made man and woman. Woman was given her space. She was free to roam the Garden. She shared responsibility with her husband. Dialogued with God. Spoke for herself. She was given an honored title—"suitable helper"—a word used twenty-one times in the Old Testament to describe God as the helper of Israel.

But then Satan came along and got her to thinking it wasn't enough.

"Come on, Eve. What do you mean, 'enough options,' when God has just crossed one off your list? What you really need is the freedom to pick and choose for yourself. You need to be able to eat from *all* the trees."

Unfortunately, Eve was taken in.

Unfortunately, we are still being taken in.

But God has a different view. From his perspective, we are enough. We have enough. "His divine power has given us everything we need for life and godliness" (2 Peter 1:3). As far as he is concerned, if we are living in obedience to him, *whatever* we are doing is enough. And *whoever* we are is enough.

The only time God looks at my efforts as insufficient is when I attempt to earn my way into his graces. Then he shakes his head sadly and says, "Sorry. Not enough."

My efforts will never be enough for God. Even with all my fancy dressing up for him, I'm still in rags (Isaiah 64:6). When I finally confess my sins, admit them to God, he says, *Now, come pull up a chair, sit down to my feast.*

So I pull up the chair. Sit down to the feast. I have come God's way. From here on out, every thought he has about me is this: "Enough."

I am doing enough. I am being enough. I *am* enough.

———

Jesus made it easy for people to be content with themselves. He was always affirming their "enough-ness." Take Mary of Bethany (Luke 10). Others didn't think she was doing enough. Even her own sister had more ambitious plans for her. But Jesus said simply, "Enough." She's doing enough. "Mary has chosen what is better" (Luke 10:42).

But poor Mary. Her accusers didn't stop with her sister. The disciples let her have it too (Mark 14).

From the disciple's perspective, breaking a bottle of expensive perfume—and an antique one at that—was just money down the drain. How financially irresponsible of

Mary! Not astute enough. Think of all the homeless who could have been fed with proceeds from the sale of her alabaster box.

But Jesus had another point of view. Enough. "She did what she could" (v. 8). Not only was it enough, it was "beautiful" (v. 6).

The Bible doesn't say Mary was a contented person. Nor does it tell us how she lived the rest of her life. But I have to believe Jesus' word "enough" had an impact. I seriously doubt that Mary drove herself to an early grave trying to establish her significance. My guess is that she lived with a sense of God's approval, and for her that was enough.

––––––

I wonder how our lives might look if we were as content with ourselves as God is with us. I wonder how different things might be if we relearned what contentment is all about. If we refused to believe we have to be something bigger, brighter, bolder than we are. If we took the pressure off ourselves by no longer having to prove ourselves significant. If we simply believed that we *are* significant.

For one thing, we would probably go about our business with greater energy. Living with great longing takes great energy. We would not rush so headlong into trying to prove ourselves. We might even take time to notice more of God—in his Word and in the world around us. And those who see us would feel our serenity. Others might even say, "There goes a woman who knows the meaning of contentment." They might even be more content with themselves by being around us.

––––––

Maybe we *have* listened too hard to the multiple voices trying to tell us exactly where it is a woman's significance lies.

Maybe we haven't listened enough for what God tells us about our worth. Maybe we need to go back to the basic book—the Bible—and track down all the verses that talk about an individual's value. Maybe we need to say to ourselves more often, "The Lord is my shepherd. I *shall not* want. Here are some things I have to be thankful for." (Thanksgiving paves the road for contentment.)

Maybe we haven't lost old-fashioned contentment forever.

Maybe, just maybe, it's not too late to claim it back.

And having done so, maybe next time we'll be more careful which voices we listen to when it comes to trying to establish our significance.

For Thought, Journaling, or Discussion:

1. How would you answer the person who says, "By telling women to be more content, we're saying they should passively accept whatever comes their way—even if it harms them"?

2. How do you as a Christian woman know when to be content with a situation and when to try to change it? What principles from God's Word apply?

3. When may contentment be a negative force? Conversely, when can discontent be good?

4. What (if any) evidences do you see that women today are less content than women may have been in the past? What do you think might be some of the causes?

5. In what ways may contentment contribute to a woman's strength?

6. How would you describe contentment? Is there a difference in Christian contentment? If so, what is it?

7. Think of a woman you would consider to be content. How do you know she is content?

8. Are you more content today than you were in the past? Why? Why not?

9. How might contentment be learned?

10. What steps do you need to take to strengthen your own contentment?

TWO

....

I have a concern about all the
archaeological digs women are on today.
We dig up grievances against men and
hang on to them as though we have no
place to deposit them.

....

What Do We Do With the Past?

Forgiveness

Anger is bubbling just beneath the surface in many women today. Mostly, it seems, we are angry at men. And the more we dig into our past, the more we find to be angry with them about.

Considering we are so intent on freedom these days, and considering there is no freedom like the freedom that comes from forgiveness, you'd think we'd be more intent on forgiving. Yet we seem to be getting more proficient at holding grudges than at rendering grace to our offenders. Our culture has taught us to stand up for ourselves. It has not taught us to lay ourselves down for one another. And until we are willing to lay ourselves down for one another, we will never learn what gracious forgiveness is all about.

Why are we in danger of losing it—this capacity to forgive and forget past offenses?

Maybe this.

During the last thirty years or so, women have done a great deal of excavating among the ancient ruins of their past. Sometimes we've uncovered treasures—the stories of women who have gone before us. Women who have been strong and courageous. Women who have lived such godly lives that they have turned the course of entire nations toward Christ. (For some examples, read about the spread of Christianity in the Roman Empire and in Britain.) Such exemplary lives give us cause for courage and hope.

But sometimes we've dug into our past and found graveyards full of abuse, injustice, oppression of all sorts. Enough to haunt us for a long, long time. Enough to make us angry for just as long.

I applaud the historian in us. Sometimes the only way to avoid the mistakes of the past is to scrutinize the past. Sometimes the only way to release the stranglehold our past has on us is to take a hard, critical look at it. Sometimes the only way to replace prejudice and misrepresentation is to unearth and study the historical facts.

But I have a concern about all the archaeological digs women are on today. We dig up grievances against men and hang on to them as though we have no place to deposit them. For Christian women this is particularly sad, because we *do* have a garbage dump for grudges and grievances. It's called forgiveness.

The kind of forgiveness I'm talking about is not human.

It's divine. It is so profound it cannot be mustered up by our own superficial efforts. So we must depend on God to work the long and arduous process of forgiveness into us. But in our newfound independence and self-sufficiency, we'd somehow rather try to muddle along for ourselves. That means we often do not get around to asking for help when it comes to forgiving.

So the chasms between men and women continue to exist—fissured out by vast forces of hostility and hatred. And we cannot seem to help ourselves out of our anger.

In the beginning, man and woman were made *for* each other. (See Genesis 2.) But time and experience has postured us more *against* than *for*. As though we need to hold each other in check, as though man is someone who is keeping us *from* something—a job, a position, a salary, the right to choose, freedom to use our gifts.

It is interesting how in my mother's day a man was seen as a woman's protector. Today, we protect ourselves *from* men. Men have become the opposition, like antagonists in a Shakespearean tragedy.

Yes, I am sadly aware that in some cases men *have been* the antagonists. Some *have* created Shakespearean tragedy for us. I shake my head in sorrow over the exploitation of women. I die a thousand deaths when I hear or know of a woman whose dignity and self-respect have died. When her body has been used. Her gifts ignored. Her work unfairly compensated. Her ideas discredited. THERE IS NO EXCUSE, I say.

There is no excuse.

But there is grace.

Grace does not *ignore* injustice. It simply chooses not to

33

hold on to it. There is a way to confront wrong with grace. In my opinion, Rosa Parks did it forty years ago when she refused to give up her seat to a white person on an Alabama bus. I don't know Rosa Parks personally and I was not there. But from what I've read, her act was not an angry lashing out of hostility, but a quiet act of conviction. From what I know of Rosa Parks today, she is not an angry woman. She has every mark of a woman of grace.

I hope the day will come when, instead of dwelling on the grievances of men, we will build monuments to the courage of women. When we will hold our conventions and talk more about all that women can be rather than about what men have done to us. I hope the day will come when men and women will lay down their swords and again become fellow pilgrims. Maybe men will then be much more to us than simply "The Opposition."

Until we forgive men their offenses, we can count on being chained forever to our past, for we can never move beyond it until we forgive. And we will never forgive without grace.

Father, forgive men (all men everywhere) their mistakes against us, as you have forgiven us our mistakes against them.

It is a prayer I've seldom heard prayed. Maybe this is why we are so preoccupied with the offenses.

Maybe it is why we are so tired. Nothing is more draining than nursing a grudge. It takes immense emotional and physical energy.

We may be tired for another reason. When we are angry with someone, we aren't about to let them do *anything* for us. We have to do it all ourselves. Not letting men help us is our way of holding them at a distance.

And some days we wear ourselves out trying to get even with men. We decide to contribute to their sufferings as much as we feel they have contributed to ours. They have ignored us. We will ignore them. They have had their flings. We will have our flings. They have devoted themselves to a career at our expense. We will devote ourselves to a career at their expense. They have pulled rank on us. We will make them pay.

Anger wears many faces. Some of us may not carry around hard-core hostilities toward men, but neither are we sympathetic toward them. We call them inept and insensitive. Their way of doing things bugs and irritates us. We put up with them. But just barely.

What we forget is this: It is as emotionally draining to be forever bugged by someone as to be forever hostile toward someone. One way or the other, our grievances against men take a great deal out of us.

Anger may also wear a passive face. On the outside we may show no symptoms, yet inside an inferno may be raging. We may bow a submissive knee, but one day the inferno will erupt. And it will take a painfully long time to sift through the debris—broken relationships, damaged spirits, terrible regret.

———

But there is an alternative to all this angry living. We can choose to let go of the wrongs done to us and to hang on to grace for all we're worth—hang on to it like a child clinging to a kite string on a windy day, always aware that at any moment our forgiving spirit can slip from our grasp. We can choose to forgive.

———

Every now and then, I get to thinking about what good, old-fashioned forgiveness really looks like. I do not have to look far for an example.

It is the early 1940s. My mother is in the process of giving birth. The delivery is unusually hard and something goes wrong. The doctor makes a judgment call. It is *not* the right call. But the damage has been done.

No one bothers to tell my mother. She has to find out for herself, and it is only a matter of months until she knows: Something is not right with her child. She also knows what is later confirmed by the specialists: It was, most likely, caused by a misjudgment on the part of the doctor.

I was not around then, so I did not see my mother's response to the news. But when I was old enough to start being curious, my mother told me the story. She related it as one would pass on the morning news—without emotion. Not one trace of blame or accusation toward the doctor.

Even today, there is not one trace of blame or accusation. And the silver baby cup Mother keeps in the corner china cabinet of her dining room says it all.

The cup is always sparkling. I read the inscription. Name. Date of birth. Weight at birth. All the information you'd expect on a silver baby cup. But it is the baby's middle name that always catches me by surprise, no matter how many times I read it. The middle name given to my brother is the last name of the doctor who delivered him.

"Why?" I ask myself.

"Why would you want to name your baby for the doctor who damaged your child?"

I know the answer: because my mother knows how to forgive.

She knows how to forgive or the silver cup would not still be around. Or she would have legally changed my brother's middle name. But the doctor's name still shines on my brother's silver baby cup.

My mother has never thought to make herself a victim. To her, the circumstances of my brother's birth are simply a matter of the less-than-perfect world we live in, where people sometimes make mistakes, even mistakes that have enormous effects on other people.

It is grace, pure and simple—the conferring of honor, respect, dignity, and love on the very person who deserves it least.

Sometimes I get to wondering whether such a concept of grace even exists anymore. Women today, it seems, have so much to blame on so many.

————

Fast forward the tape fifty years. My mother is in the hospital again, this time for a routine heart procedure.

"Should take care of the problem," the doctor says. "We do the procedure all the time."

But the procedure does not take care of the problem. In fact, it creates a crisis that almost takes my mother's life. She is rushed into a six-hour surgery. She does not open her eyes for five days and does not leave the hospital for thirty. When she is finally discharged, she knows it is only a temporary respite. Three weeks and she will be back for another surgery and a recuperation even more strenuous than the first.

Two thoughts hammer my brain during the long days and nights of my mother's crisis—two thoughts at war with each other: God is in control, BUT it *was* the doctor's fault.

Lord, deliver me from hating the doctor.

Sometimes the prayer works. Sometimes it doesn't.

My mother is struggling for life. I, for forgiveness.

"Your mother is a woman of great strength and courage,"

the doctor says to me one morning in the hallway outside her room.

I tell my mother what her doctor has said. She smiles weakly.

"Doctor _____ is a very special man," she says. "Yesterday, he ordered me French toast with maple syrup for breakfast. I'm still supposed to be eating oatmeal, but I told him French toast with maple syrup was my favorite breakfast."

My mother is not naive. She knows, as we all do, that her crisis was most likely caused by human error. But I am struck by the fact that my mother has chosen to forget the doctor's mistake, and remembers instead that he ordered her French toast with maple syrup when she was supposed to be eating oatmeal.

Two years have passed. My mother's body has never fully recouped what it lost to that "routine procedure." She still faithfully visits the same doctor for checkups. I call to see how the visit went. In almost every phone call, my mother has some good word for her doctor. How devoted he seems to be to his family and his patients. How often he asks her about her family. (She has never forgotten that he called me halfway across the country to give me a firsthand report during some of my more anxious hours when I could not be by my mother's side.)

"Doctor _____ is a special man."

My mother really believes it.

It is grace, pure and simple.

It keeps my mother from becoming an angry woman. Or a whining woman. Or a helpless woman who is forever tossed about by someone's injustice or ineptitude toward her.

———

I look within me. I seldom find such sterling grace.

I look around me. I seldom see such grace around me.

Oh yes, we know the social skills of gracious living. We've gotten good at grace on the outside, not so good at grace on the inside—grace that enables us to forgive and forget past offenses, grace that moves us on to liberation of the spirit.

———

Where, then, do we begin if we would move toward forgiveness?

We don't begin by coming together in corporate prayer, telling God that once and for all we forgive the entire male population. Amen. And so be it. (Forgiveness is not so simple a matter.)

Forgiveness must begin with me—one person, forgiving one man: the one who has wronged me or shortchanged me or made me suffer or bugged me . . . or whatever.

I do not wait until I have the wherewithal to forgive. In fact, forgiveness can best begin when I *know* I don't have what it takes to forgive.

Lord, there is not an ounce of grace in me to forgive this person. I don't even want to forgive him. So you will have to pour the grace into me—and keep pouring it into me.

Forgiveness must begin whether I feel like it or not. Somewhere along the line I must tell my head what my heart does not feel: There *is* something right about this person who has caused me so much pain. I may not be able to think of anything. But somewhere, sometime, there is something right about everyone. So I must dig for the good. (I am probably already well into my dig for the bad.)

Maybe I need to talk to someone who knew the person before I did. Or someone who knows him from a different place. As absurd as it may seem, I may need to try to picture him as some mother's son. (That's bound to do a little softening of my heart.)

If I'm having trouble forming a mind-picture of this person doing good, I may need to draw the picture on paper. *If he were to do something kind for me, what might it look like?* Or I may need to write a story about it and read it to someone. However I do it, I must get the possibility into my brain: This person may not be all bad.

Forgiveness gives the benefit of the doubt. It looks for reasons why, like a detective looking for clues. What was my offender's childhood like? Did his father ever compliment him? Did his mother give him hugs and kisses? Did his friends ridicule him? Have his dreams gone sour? Has someone abused him? Disappointed him? Walked out on him?

Maybe there will be clues and maybe there won't. I may have to come to the place where I say simply, "I don't understand this person. But I choose forgiveness anyhow."

Once I have begun to tread this personal trail to forgiveness, I will find there is also a road for me to walk with all women everywhere. I must find grace not only for an individual's offense but also for a culture's offenses. I will no doubt read the history books, uncovering all sorts of injustices. All well and good that I read history, as long as I read it with grace firmly in my heart. Without grace, history has potential for making me a bitter woman.

History will record certain sermons, certain books. I will read the record and say, "Wait a minute here. There *is* another side." All well and good, as long as I make such statements with grace firmly in my heart. Without grace, disagreement quickly turns to hostility.

Some of the things I read or learn about the past may have such a drastic effect on me that I cannot get over it by myself. Calling for help is the sensible thing to do. But once I have tried to make sense of it, once I have dealt with the emotion of it (whether on my own or with the help of another), then I ultimately must make a choice to get over it. Having opened the history book, I must at some point also close it, put it back on the shelf, and get on with living.

We must encourage one another to get on with living. Yes, we must listen sympathetically. Give advice, or lead another to someone who can. But always, we must point each other toward forgiveness.

Sometimes a woman may be so angry she cannot even pray for strength to forgive. Then we must pray for her. We are no good to anyone when we simply say, "Poor thing. You've had it hard. How awful of him!" When we don't point others toward forgiveness, we leave them in worse shape than we found them. When we don't point them toward forgiveness, we leave their exposed wound uncovered. The most loving thing we can do for them is to help them wrap the hurt in forgiveness.

Forgiving calls for courage. It calls for humility. But perhaps most of all it calls for us to step up and take responsibility for ourselves.

Oh, but it is so much easier to blame someone else. *He made me do it!* As though we were still children, looking for an excuse. But we are not children. And we need to outgrow our excuses.

It is good to practice owning up to ourselves now, because it is what we will have to do someday when we face God. "So then, each of us will give an account of [herself] to God" (Romans 14:12.) God will not ask us how people have treated us before he makes his judgment call. He will ask us about *us*.

A life without forgiveness comes to a sad end. Without forgiveness, hopelessness sets in. And if hopelessness sets in, we will become bitter old women who sit and stare out the window, filling space with our anger, waiting defiantly for whatever life will inflict upon us next.

But forgiveness keeps us hopeful. *We can change. We can take responsibility for our responses. We can grab on to life and make it what God wants it to be. Enough of this being pushed around by our own anger.* And when that happens we will be able to take the injustices of our past, as awful as they may seem, and craft them into pure gold—learning compassion from them; learning honest, loving confrontation; learning about truthfulness and integrity in our relationships with men.

Then *we* will be the example of grace and others will know: Here is what forgiveness looks like.

For Thought, Journaling, or Discussion:

1. What would you say to someone who says, "Women today have a right to be angry"?
2. Do you see signs of anger in women today? If so, where do they show up?
3. What do you think might be at the heart of this anger?
4. Can anger ever work for us? Why or why not?
5. What does Scripture teach about anger? (Check out Exodus 34:6; 2 Chronicles 24:18–19; Job 9:13; Psalms 4:4, 30:5, 37:8, 103:8–9; Proverbs 15:1, 27:4, 29:8, 11, 30:33; Romans 2:8–11; Ephesians 4:26–27; 1 Timothy 2:8; James 1:20.)
6. What would you say to someone who says that all anger is sin?
7. Write down an example of a time when anger affected your relationship with a man. How was your relationship affected? How were you able to work through the anger?
8. If you have not worked through the anger, where might you begin? Write down a first step.
9. How might anger be affecting your view of men in general?
10. What steps might you take to deal with this kind of anger?

THREE

....

Something is badly wrong with the notion that for Christian women there is one way and only one way to fill a role.

....

Waning Signs of Sisterhood

Unity

Christian sisterhood has turned on itself. Our unity is fraying at the seams. The rhetoric against one another is getting stronger, and the idea of "Christian sisters united" that looked so good on paper not long ago is beginning to sour. We are stuck trying to figure out why.

Why *are* Christian women so hard on other women these days, given our claims to be so open-minded? Why are we so critical of other women's ways of doing things, especially when we profess such Christian charity? Why, despite all our coming together in the last thirty years, are we in such splinters? So inflexible in our opinions? So down on women who see and do things differently?

It is a strange turn of events, this disunity infecting us, especially in light of all we know. We are so skilled in the ways of human behavior, so well-versed in relational matters, so up-to-date about family dynamics, so knowledgeable about our faith and theology.

You'd think sisterhood—especially among Christian women—would be blossoming. But then maybe all our knowledge is part of the problem. Perhaps we know so much we've become inflexible. Our theories and our interpretations may be threatening our Christian tolerance for one another.

Maybe all the growing and developing we've done as individuals makes us snub our noses at those who haven't had those same growth spurts—at other women we consider not quite as far along in their "spiritual maturity" as we are. Maybe it also has to do with chronological age. Maybe we criticize the way younger women do things because we forget what it was like to be young. Maybe we are quick to judge older women because we haven't taken time to think about what it might be like to be on that end of life. Maybe we forget that many things change at different ages and stages of our lives. Perhaps that is another reason we've become intolerant of one another.

———

I am in a new season of life. I'm a different woman in midlife than I was in my great gusto, go-for-it, child-rearing years. Then I took life in great gulps. Now I have to take time to chew and digest all those big bites I was taking back then.

It is a quieter season. I find myself turning inward a bit more. Becoming more reflective. Focusing more on what it is

I really want to do with the rest of my life. Exploring the depths at home rather than scouting about, further afield.

It is a satisfying season for me. But sometimes I hear a note of alarm in another's voice. *You're not doing* _____ *anymore! What a shame!*

And then, though no one ever says it, I can imagine the thought: *Poor Ruth. She's dying on the vine. And just when she has all this time on her hands.*

How I spend my time depends on the season of my life.

How I mother, for example, depends on the seasons of my children's lives. I had my office in the guest bedroom when my children were still home all day and built Lego cities under my typewriter while I wrote. When my children went away to college, I moved my office to a corporate headquarters, where I could make a more significant contribution to my children's college fund. I am cutting back on my work load now that they have graduated and are on their own.

I am mothering long-distance these days. I spend time talking on the phone to my children, friend to friend, less time advising and consulting. I'm back to some of the personal pursuits I put on hold when the children came along. Back to browsing the local library for the sheer pleasure of it, to dusting off my piano skills, to poking through flea markets, and to reading all those biographies I've collected over the years but never had time to read.

My marriage has changed with the seasons. I took a more aggressive role in decision-making when my husband traveled a lot, the children were still home, and there were a hundred and one on-the-spot decisions that had to be made. Now that we have long dinner and evening hours together, just the two of us, we have more time to discuss and come to consensus.

Since our dinner conversation is now two-way instead of four-way, we are also much more informed about what the other person is doing. With fewer children's activities to attend, we attend more of each other's activities. We share more of the household tasks now that the children aren't around to help. It is a luxurious time of marriage—of life—even with all the brown spots appearing on my hands and the creaks in my knees when I bend to get something from a bottom shelf.

The truth of the seasons of our lives is not that one season is more right than another or more productive or more biblical. It is simply that one season is different from another.

How tragic if we allow the seasons of our lives to become the great divide among women, failing to take into account that women do things differently according to their particular season.

I long for the day when the estrogen generation will find best friends among "The Xers" and "The Busters" will sit down to coffee with the Medicare crowd. And across the seasons, everyone will learn from one another. Everyone will enjoy one another.

———

It's what happened last summer when my mother, my daughter, my friend, and I traveled England for ten days. There was diversity right from the start.

We were coming together from three different states and a foreign country.

We represented three different seasons of life. My daughter is in her mid-twenties. My mother, nearly eighty. My friend and I—well, we're mid-life.

We are at different stages of our careers.

My daughter is a sales representative for a large publishing house. Her husband is about to graduate from university. My friend is beginning her dissertation for a Ph.D. after having taught for twenty-some years. My mother is about to celebrate fifty years of pastoral ministry with my dad. And I'm beginning work on a new book, having recently "retired" from the magazine business.

We are at different stages of our mothering.

My friend and I are both mothers of two adult children. I am mother-in-law of one. My mother is mother of five, grandmother of ten, great-grandmother of two. And my daughter has a cat.

Our husbands warned us of the risks of our great diversity.

Remember, you will be the outsider. Three family members and you.

Remember, you will be the outsider. Three older women and you.

Remember, you will be the outsider. Three younger women and you.

Remember, you will be the outsider. Three non-Anglophiles and you.

But it worked—all this diversity. In fact, we entered into one another's diversity.

When Grandma needed to slow down and rest for the sake of her heart, we all slowed down and rested. When one of us wanted a McDonald's hamburger (guess which one), we all ate McDonald's hamburgers. When one of us wanted to see London on-stage, we all walked London's Strand and went to the theater.

We were an assorted lot, yes, except for this shared experience—England.

We laughed and cried. We ate and slept. Roamed the Cotswolds—gardens, market towns, medieval castles, palaces, old churches, quiet country lanes. The sights and sounds and tastes of England brought us together. We were a unit, solid and tight.

And we came home friends. In fact, we came home better friends, because now there are no illusions about one another.

That trip gave me great hope for women everywhere.

We *can* come together in our diversity. There can be learning and enjoying and supporting, even across the dissimilarities.

———

How tragic when differences get in the way. How especially sad when our Christian ideologies and biblical interpretations keep us apart.

Something is badly wrong with the notion that for Christian women there is one way and only one way to fill a role. I have my convictions about how I should live my life. My convictions are based upon obvious requirements laid out for me in the Bible—requirements laid out for every disciple of Christ, be they male or female. For example, as one who follows Christ, I am to always put another's welfare before my own. That means I will always be willing to sacrifice for the sake of another. I will be loyal. I will be honest. I will draw on God's Word and his wisdom for every decision. But within the basic parameters governing God's will for my life, there is large room for variation.

I trust the day will come when Christian women can bury the hatchet over such issues as whether a mother should work inside or outside the home. I look forward to the time when go-to-work moms will no longer be convinced that all stay-at-home moms are denying their God-given gifts, when stay-at-home moms will concede that not all go-to-work moms are denying their God-given responsibilities.

I trust we will soon give up on trying to oversee one another's lives.

I trust the day will come when we will not make issues of things Scripture does not make issues of—like where a woman works.

Despite all our debates, I see no catagorical command in Scripture: *Women should never, on any occasion, work outside the home.* In fact, Scripture gives examples of women whose usefulness to God extended beyond the home. Priscilla taught (Acts 18); Miriam prophesied and lead the women of Israel in worship (Exodus 15); Philip's daughters prophesied (Acts 21:9); Anna was a prophetess (Luke 2:36); Deborah led Israel as a judge, a prophetess, a military commander (Judges 4). Even "The Virtuous Woman" of Proverbs 31—whether she was one woman or a composite of many—could not possibly have pursued all her endeavors inside the four walls of her home (especially in a day without E-mail and fax machines).

I trust the day will come when we will emphasize godly, Christlike living rather than what a woman can and cannot do with her roles; when we will do what Jesus did—look to the heart of people rather than stand and point fingers at what they are or are not doing. (Check out Matthew 23 for Jesus' strong condemnation of people who emphasized the wrong things.) I trust the day will come when we will take Jesus' words to heart: "If you had known what these words mean, 'I desire mercy, not sacrifice,' you would not have condemned the innocent" (Matthew 12:7). Jesus spoke this to the Pharisees, who were nit-picking that the disciples had, contrary to the law, plucked some grain for their breakfast on the Sabbath.

———

Agreed, it is a rather frightening time for Christian

women. And maybe we are so hard on each other because we don't yet know what all the outcomes of this "new day for women" will be. We are afraid we will lose what we ought to hang on to. We *need* to be afraid of losing what we should be keeping. But I pray the day will come when a bad case of the jitters is no longer an excuse for our intolerance. Uncertain times should send us to our knees for one another, not into the arena, like lions waiting to pounce on one another.

The older generation of women didn't seem so jittery about how other women did things. True, there were not as many different ways to be a woman back then. But in that less complicated time they learned the great virtue of simply taking other women in, despite their differences in style. Maybe when life was harder women didn't have time or energy to sit around and criticize each other.

The older generation has taught me something important about coming together despite the differences.

My mother doesn't usually ride with motorcycle gangs. But this morning she does—not on a motorcycle but in a hearse with Daddy and the undertaker. A cavalcade of twenty motorcycles follow the hearse at a respectful distance, as though not to waken the dead.

It is a world beyond my mother's world. But funeral processions have a way of bringing people together, of weaving them, despite their differences, into a mournful line to the cemetery. The toughness of the crowd does not appear to have bothered my mother.

I think, as Mother tells me the story: She *could* have decided not to go into the cold February weather for this group of strangers so unlike herself. Only one small thread tied her to them. She knew the grandmother of the dead man. The grandmother was the only one in the family who knew a preacher, and she asked my father to do the service. But that still did not commit my mother.

Someone less stouthearted than my nearly eighty-year-old mother would have stayed home and cared for herself. One less tolerant of differences would simply have closed the door. *Let them feel for themselves. They live for themselves.*

Why did my mother go? I cannot say. But I can say this: How another woman dressed or looked or grieved or rode to the cemetery did not seem to matter to my mother. She was there for a woman who was about to commit a grandson to the grave. Although my mother probably would not have recognized it as such, her story sounded a lot like what I dream of sisterhood being.

Sisterhood: where coming alongside is more important than issuing a critique.

Sisterhood: where we use our intellect to think of ways to bring us together, not further divide.

It is high time we use reason, rather than sheer emotion, to address the issues that divide. It is time we lay off the answers for a while and listen to some of the questions women struggle with today.

I hope the day will come when we will lay aside our biases long enough to see what the Bible does and does not say. When our preconceived notions will no longer get in the way. When we will ponder more what it means to live with love, joy, peace, patience, kindness, goodness, faithfulness, gentleness, and self-control firmly attached to our lives (Galatians 5:22), and pontificate less on what a woman can or cannot do.

I suspect we might find, to our surprise, that if we are living by the fruit of the Spirit and are taking up our cross daily and following Christ (Matthew 10:38), we will know beyond a shadow of a doubt what we should and should not be doing, and we will have the common sense to allow other women to do the same.

What would it be like if we came together in true Christian sisterhood?

Maybe we wouldn't be so judgmental of women who interpret Scripture's teaching about women's roles a little differently than we do. Maybe we would not write them off or seek to discredit them.

Maybe we wouldn't be so jealous of others' successes. Maybe when another woman soars to the top professionally, we would not try to come up with all the reasons why she shouldn't be there.

She will ruin her marriage if she makes more money than her husband.

She will raise juvenile delinquents if she becomes a vice-president.

She will wreck her home if she travels across the country from time to time.

She will end up divorced if she gets more publicity than her husband.

While all of the above are possibilities, not all are givens. We would be far more helpful to one another if we prayed for God's protection on our sisters rather than trying to do the protecting ourselves.

May God deliver us from paranoia.

And may God deliver us from resenting others' successes.

If anyone could have been jealous of another's success, it

was Elizabeth. Elizabeth was an older woman of wisdom. A voice of experience. She was a pastor's wife, known throughout the hill country of Judea as godly and upright. She was a woman who thought and spoke for herself. And besides all this, she was a descendant of Aaron—of the priestly class (See Luke 1).

She was as likely a pick as any to be the mother of the Messiah.

In fact, she was probably even more likely than most. She had all the right qualifications.

But God did not promote Elizabeth. He promoted Mary.

Little Mary. (Barely a teenager.) No experience. Not officially married, and carrying a child. (In those days, an offense punishable by stoning.) What did Mary know about life? She had no proper credentials to be the mother of the Lord.

Had I been Elizabeth, I'm not sure I would so graciously have taken Mary in when she came knocking on my door. *How shameful, to come boasting of your pregnancy before your marriage is official!*

But Elizabeth opened not only her door to Mary. She opened her heart. She sang Mary's praises: "Blessed are you among women, and blessed is the child you will bear! But why am I so favored, that the mother of my Lord should come to me?" (Luke 1:42–43).

If we practiced true sisterhood, we might be more likely to celebrate one another's promotions, whether we think they are merited or not.

If we practiced true sisterhood, we might give one another room to relate to men in different ways.

But we are so full of opinions.

Women should submit.

Women should exert themselves.

Women should be under a man's authority.
Women should be equals.
Women should obey.
Women should be their own person.
Women should speak up.
Women should shut up.
Women should take initiative.
Women should follow suit.

There are so many opinions our heads are swimming. Every opinion has its scripture verse to go with it. And every verse has its Greek words with more than one meaning. But still we say, *In no uncertain terms, here's how the Lord thinks you should be relating to men, spending your days, caring for your children.*

Whatever happened to the day when we allowed one another to ask, *Lord, what do YOU want me to do?*

For a woman, there has always been more than one way to fill her roles. In Scripture, it is true. Across the world, in different cultures, it is true. From ages past, it has been true. And it is still true today.

Maybe if we practiced true sisterhood, we would admit there are different ways for a Christian woman to fill a role.

Maybe if we practiced true sisterhood, we would not eyeball each other to scrutinize how another woman relates to a man. Maybe we would not be so quick to sit behind our desk or stand behind our sink and criticize. *She's selling out. She's playing games. She's flirting. She's competing. She's brown-nosing. She's being co-dependent. She's power-brokering. She's being a doormat.*

––––––––

Maybe, if we truly believed in Christian sisterhood, we

would give women room to relate differently to men. We would recognize that some women are more comfortable sitting back and letting men do all the talking. Some women don't mind if men earn the money, negotiate with the plumber, and balance the checkbook. On the other hand, some *men* don't want to be burdened with those details and wouldn't know where to start if they did. Maybe, if we truly believed in sisterhood, we would be quicker to say, "That's okay, if that works best in your marriage." Maybe we would see that some personalities are quieter than others. Some, by nature, are simply more take-charge.

If we truly believed in sisterhood, we would truly practice sisterhood. We would go looking for women who are not at all like us, then try to get to know them so that we could better understand who they are and why they act the way they do. We would ask them questions rather than try to hand them answers. We would talk: *What have been your greatest struggles as a Christian woman? Your greatest joys?* We would even get around to asking the greatest servant question of all: *What can I do to help make your load lighter?*

Time was, we could gather round a quilting frame and spend the day getting to know one another. But since now there is not much chance of that, we will have to find another way. Like having our neighbors in for coffee, volunteering at a crisis pregnancy center, or serving on one of our town's commissions, or joining a civic organization or a garden club, or playing in the local symphony.

We need to look for each other in places where we find women least like ourselves—that is, if we truly want to close the gaps that exist between us. Maybe when we get around to knowing each other we won't find so much to condemn.

Spending time together does not mean we will agree, or

even that we *should* agree. But if Christian sisterhood is going to revive itself, it will have to get over its fear of disagreement over women's roles. It will have to learn to listen carefully, to offer up convictions with great humility, and then say, *I see it quite differently, but still, I value you and your right to your opinion.*

We may not leave each other having become the best of friends. In fact, we probably won't. But that's okay. We do not have to be best of friends, only sympathetic sisters.

For it seems to me that is what the notion of Christian sisterhood is all about. We will not see things the same way when it comes to our roles. We will not do things the same way. But we *will* be loyal to each other. We *will* look for gifts to affirm in each other. We *will* devote every ounce of energy in us, to see not only that men give women a fair shake but that *we* give women a fair shake.

For it is time we learn once again how to come together in our diversity and then stick by each other, no matter what.

For Thought, Journaling, or Discussion:

1. What things do you see causing division among Christian women today?

2. What are some of the results of these divisions? Do you think these results are healthy or unhealthy for women? Harmful or helpful to the body of Christ?

3. Does being tolerant of another woman's viewpoints about women's roles mean you have no convictions of your own? Why or why not?

4. Does the Bible give any guidelines for how to balance holding to your convictions while still being tolerant of another's? If so, what are they?

5. If you really believe your biblical view of women is right, doesn't that imply that all others are wrong? How then do you let your views be known in a Christlike way? Or should you just keep them to yourself?

6. Do you agree or disagree with this statement: "We have made a bigger issue out of a woman's role than God does"? If you disagree, how would you respond to the woman making the statement?

7. If you agreed with the above statement, obviously you will disagree with this statement: "God makes it completely clear how women should fill their roles." How would you respond to a woman making that statement?

8. What steps could women in your circles take to help close the gaps with women of other "circles"?

9. What are some steps you personally need to take?

10. When it comes to Christian women who hold views differing from yours about Scripture's teaching on women, what attitudes do you need to ask God to help you with?

FOUR

·················

Now that we can dream big dreams, we are so in a hurry to get to them—as though we have to realize them all tomorrow, as though they are soap bubbles, a squeeze of the hand and they will be gone. Our dreams have become our frenzy.

·················

The Serious Business of Being a Woman

Humor

I would expect women today to be more lighthearted. Never have we had it so easy. I'd expect to see us casting aside our cares and helping ourselves to a healthy dose of cheer more often. You'd think with all our trips and vacations and eating out and watching games, plays, movies, concerts—we'd have more deep-down exuberance.

But I see women with furrowed brows, tension etched in the set of the jaw. I see us looking straight ahead when we walk, fixed on where we're going and how much time we have to get there. Women don't smile as much these days.

Maybe it takes too much time to smile. Maybe it is too feminine to smile. Who will take you seriously if you go around smiling all the time? Maybe smiling women finish last.

I worry about this new intensity I see in us today. I wonder where it all will lead.

———

For one, it surely has led to a life without much laughter. I am sorry I don't laugh more often.

I'm sorry women today don't laugh more often. That we seem to have traded in our lightheartedness for such weight.

Though there's good reason for this.

Take our increased responsibilities, for example. We have added duty upon duty, role upon role. Career upon career. We are multileveled in our obligations.

Added to that is the fact that we are only thirty or so years into the new ordering of our lives. We are still finding our way. Our jobs (be they in-house or out-of-house) are as much preoccupation as occupation. They very nearly "rule" our days (and sometimes our nights).

And now that we can dream big dreams, we are so in a hurry to get to them—as though we have to realize them all tomorrow, as though they are soap bubbles, a squeeze of the hand and they will be gone. Our dreams have become our frenzy.

No wonder we live with such intensity.

Women today tend to live as though EVERYTHING matters, as though a hundred years from now EVERYTHING will *still* matter.

I wonder.

I wonder whether everything that feels like A BIG DEAL really is a big deal. Perhaps women today have gotten so used to handling BIG DEALS we don't know how to handle little deals anymore—an interesting conundrum since a woman's life is made up of so much detail.

Maybe we've forgotten how to allow for trivialities.

No wonder we feel such weight.

The trouble is that in all our taking on of additional duties and responsibilities, we have not taken on additional cheer to balance them out. Maybe this is why we wear such serious faces.

I am very aware: This *is* serious business women are about today. It calls for great concentration to juggle all our commitments. We have to be one mental step ahead of ourselves. Always. We have a lot on our minds. We carefully weigh all our options. We take on the weight.

I guess I'm not really surprised we aren't smiling more these days.

And then too, we fear being seen as "frivolous" females. The last thing we want to do is to keep that myth alive by overdosing on levity. We aim to bury the stereotype. Unfortunately, we might be burying our humor along with it. Life is reduced to raw grit and determination—a pretty bland existence, it seems to me.

Don't get me wrong. I'm glad women today are about serious business. And yes, if we want to be taken seriously, we have to *be* serious. There is no merit to the giddy-schoolgirl approach to life. I'm glad our works *are* weighty. They should be. I'm thankful we realize it's not fun and games that make us credible sources. It is more like blood, guts, and gore. I'm glad we've come to a new awareness of that in recent years.

I am not concerned about our serious side. We desperately need it.

But I am concerned that we no longer have a light side.

I think we stand to be the losers for it.

When our light side is gone, dark becomes our way of seeing. Like wearing sunglasses on a gray day, the scene is doubly bleak. The world as it is. And the world as we see it. We open ourselves to perpetual gloom.

Lightheartedness is the balance we need. Left to ourselves, our thoughts usually go toward the dark side. If we could stack our depressing thoughts next to our sunny thoughts, most likely depressing thoughts would win. (Especially if it's January or February and you live where it's cold.)

Seems to me there is already enough heaviness of spirit in the world without our taking on more. Gravity pulls at our faces. One must give conscious thought toward reversing the flow. A sense of humor might help.

So might learning to laugh at ourselves again.

I wonder if women are having a harder time laughing at themselves these days. Okay. Let me be more personal. I wonder if I'm having a harder time laughing at myself these days.

———

I am not sorry that I take my work so seriously.

I am sorry that I take myself so seriously.

There was nothing better for my ego than that morning, several years ago, when I woke up to one of the biggest events I'd ever been invited to and realized the store where I'd bought my new dress for the occasion had mistakenly packed the same dress I'd bought, only two sizes bigger. I was a thousand miles from home (and the store), and the event started an hour from the time of discovery!

Sad to say, I did not laugh. But I did wear the dress. And after the event had long come and gone and I found out how much fun could be had by telling the story, my only regret was that I hadn't laughed sooner. I would probably remember more of the actual event today—and less about how I felt—had I laughed sooner.

Think how healthy it would be for us if we remembered how to laugh at ourselves. Think how healthy it would be for the people around us. It might loosen *them* up too. They might finally be able to admit that it's just a matter of time until something just as embarrassing happens to them.

We must get over this idea that the whole world is watching us, that the whole world is laughing at us. It's a very ego-centered thought. The truth is no one much knows whether our dress is two sizes too big or not. No one much cares. (Most people are too busy worrying about their own outfit.) So we might as well relax and enjoy ourselves. Better yet, we might as well laugh.

We will never be able to laugh at ourselves as long as we feel we are being laughed *at*. I'm not sure, but I suspect people who feel they *are* the joke don't read the funny pages in the morning newspaper either.

Maybe as women we aren't quite comfortable yet when the lights are on us. We don't quite know what to do with our hands. One wrong move and people might start laughing.

And maybe we are still trying to prove ourselves adequate. Maybe our secret fear is still that we will be discovered for our incompetency—never mind there are signs all around of our new capabilities. Maybe we have yet to convince ourselves.

So women must do some restructuring of their thoughts these days.

Self, we must say, *you are not a laughing matter. You are competent. Remember what you have accomplished. Remember the trust others have put in you.*

Those thoughts might help us put our self-doubts to bed so that we won't be so afraid of ourselves.

————

I long for the day we will be able to smile again. When we can laugh at ourselves more freely. When we won't have to try so hard. When we won't have so much to prove. When we can lighten up.

Seems to me, there was also a time when women sang more often. For no apparent reason.

Take my mother, for example. She sang. She still sings today. I don't mean stand up in church, choose one of four parts—alto, soprano, tenor, bass—and then belt it out. My mother is an alto and she has a lovely voice, but that's not the kind of singing I'm talking about.

My mother sings in the kitchen—of all places!!

For as long as I can remember, my mother has been singing in the kitchen. It is one of my most vivid childhood memories.

I am just waking up. The sun is splashing against the pink walls of my room. The birds are singing outside my window and my mother is singing in the kitchen—just the other side of my bedroom door. It is enough to make a child want to get up, face the day, and join in the fun.

I don't sing. I couldn't find a harmony part if my life depended on it—unless I'm standing next to someone who has already found a part. Oh yes, I sing in church when the congregation sings. And I have on occasion sung in a choir where I could be secure in the fact that everyone within a six-foot radius is singing the same part as I am.

But even if I *could* sing, I wonder if I *would* sing. And an even more ponderous question: Would I sing in the kitchen? Would I have something to sing about?

Knowing me, I would spend half the day trying to decide if I had anything to sing about. And by the time I had settled that question, I probably couldn't think of anything appropriate to sing.

Maybe we think too much today. Maybe we have become too calculated about it all. I don't think singing ever was or is today a cognitive activity with my mother. She just sings. The notes just bubble out, which means they are bubbling inside somewhere. She doesn't seem to need a reason for her singing.

My mother whistles too. Although I have not heard her whistling a lot recently—maybe when you are nearly eighty you need your breath for other things—I do remember vividly her whistling days of the past. All this sent a message to me as a child. Mother is happy. She likes what she's doing. She enjoys her life. She is at peace. Mother's singing and whistling were great security for me. Cheered me by day. Comforted me by night. Especially when I had to walk in the dark through the back gate and along the edge of the cotton field to the outhouse. I always liked Mother to go along because she whistled all the way.

While she may not whistle as much today, she still *does* know how to laugh. She laughs with her whole body. She laughs so hard she cries. When she starts laughing everyone ends up laughing, no matter how gloomy they might have been before.

Mother has always laughed. I remember one childhood dinnertime in particular. The wing of our drop-leaf table—loaded with food, dishes and all—fell. It dumped everything right onto Mother's and Daddy's laps. I was probably no more than ten or so at the time, but I will never forget the scene. We all looked at Mother in shock. The mess sprawled out before us—the food, Mother's bright yellow, green, orange, and blue

Fiesta dishes, all jumbled there in laps and on the floor.

We took our cues from Mother. When she started laughing, we all started laughing. And we didn't stop laughing until the sun went down later that night. Every time Mother thought of the table wing falling, she started laughing. And every time she started laughing, we all started laughing. It was the merriest of nights.

Today, my mother is still laughing about something. She could not part with laughter any more than she could part with her brown eyes.

She laughs tonight when I call her. She and Daddy have just come home from a fund-raising dinner. They had to drive through snowdrifts higher than their car to get there. (The East, where they live, is digging itself out of thirty-one inches of snow.)

"And there were golden halos around everything tonight—" my mother says, "the cars we passed on the road, the people at the dinner!" She laughs. "It was a heavenly night!"

We enjoy the moment together. I know she is referring to the effects of the drops the doctor put in her eyes earlier in the day. Mother had cataract surgery last fall and lives with a deteriorating condition in her right eye. I also know the doctor's drops make her nauseous. She doesn't mention the nausea, but she does laugh about the halos.

I wonder how bad Mother's eyes might be had she chosen not to be a laughing person.

––––––––

Not only do I long for the day when we will help ourselves to a healthy dose of laughter more often, I long for the day when our disappointments will not weigh so heavily on us. The Lord knows we have had our share of disappointment.

No one's life is as magical as they once thought it would be. If there is one thing we learn as we grow older, it is this: "You've got to walk this lonesome valley. You've got to walk it by yourself. Nobody else can walk it for you. You've got to walk it by yourself."

The song is not just a song about death. It is also a song about life.

No matter how closely I walk with God, no matter how closely I walk with friends and family, the reality is: I am on my own. No one else lives my days or sleeps my nights. No one else makes my decisions, cries my tears, laughs my joys, speaks my words, thinks my thoughts. No one else shoulders my day-in, day-out responsibilities. I walk it alone. And sometimes that can feel very solitary.

But it is life. And the sooner we embrace the "lonesome valley" concept, the less power our disappointments will have over us. It is when we expect perpetual mountaintops that we set ourselves up for despair. When we expect the valley, anything else is a pure bonus.

A bleak existence?

Maybe not.

Maybe the sooner we buy into this view of life—that life is not perpetual happiness—the greater the possibility that joy will break through.

I say "joy" because joy is the only word I can think of for what happens when heaviness lifts in the midst of our disappointments. We can laugh on our own. We cannot become a fountain of joy on our own. Any light that breaks through disappointment (grief, sorrow, pain, whatever . . .) has got to be God's doing, not ours.

The miracle of joy is this: It happens when there is no apparent reason for it. Circumstances may call for despair. Yet something different rouses itself inside us. The heaviness lifts. We are able to remember what the sunrise looks like. We feel our faces softening, our muscles relaxing. Most of all, we remember God. We remember he is love. We remember he is near.

We have known lightheartedness in the midst of disappointment.

We have known joy.

———

While we cannot create joy on our own, we can help it along.

For instance: You are alone. Very alone. Loneliness fills every corner of your empty house. Left to yourself, things would stay that way. You do not want to help yourself. You only want to feel sorry for yourself.

But somewhere further down inside you, you remember something. It is a scrap of recollection—maybe a conversation, a quote, a caption on a billboard. You're not sure what has brought it to your mind, but it is there anyway.

In your loneliness, maybe what you remember is something like this: "You don't have to have company to throw a party."

You shake yourself. You light a candle. You get busy in the kitchen, bake a quiche, and then arrange it on a plate the way a food editor would for a magazine picture. But you're not doing it for a magazine picture, you are doing it for you. You build a fire in the fireplace, put on Handel's *Water Music,* curl up with a favorite book.

Human efforts, to be sure, but a cradle for the rebirth of joy.

Considering all the circumstances, joy should not have broken through.

But it did.

And suddenly you know what the spiritual side of light-heartedness is all about.

You have known the miracle of joy.

———

I long for the day when we can look away from ourselves and our miseries long enough for that kind of joy to happen, when we learn to give ourselves up to God so joy can find us.

The tragedy is that we work so hard at joy. Like everything else, it becomes another of our intensities, as though if we study it with enough diligence, we will certainly begin to feel it; as though if we reflect upon it long enough, we will certainly bring it to pass.

Yet joy is elusive. It comes from within, but can't be produced from within. It flows most freely when we stop trying to make it happen. We do not come to joy. Joy comes to us.

Maybe we stand to lose joy today because, like everything else, we go after it so hard. Maybe because we have become so philosophical about it.

I have done my fair share of expostulating on the subject of joy. I have taught the book of Philippians (Paul's journey toward joy) more than any book in the Bible. I learned much through my study. But studying joy did not produce the effect in me. Joy doesn't work that way.

I have known joy the most when I have gone after it the least.

Like the water Jesus promised to the Samaritan woman, joy has been "a spring of water welling up . . ." (John 4:14). I could not help it. Joy simply flowed. I did not know how. Or even why. But I did know it was God's doing, not mine. That was enough.

Maybe the sooner we forget about finding joy, the sooner we will stumble upon it. Maybe the harder we go after God, the sooner we will find joy, for joy is always somewhere along the road when we have our sights set on God.

I long for the day we will be so looking for God that we will stumble on joy quite by accident.

I long for the day we will return to the place where, for the first time, joy became a possibility.

Certainly there was no appearance of joy that day when darkness fell over Jerusalem in the middle of the afternoon. Women stood at the base of the wooden crossbeam and cried. But in the midst of that darkness, joy was born. Burdens were lifted for all time and eternity.

The burden of sin, yes. It is what the Cross is all about.

But also the weight.

The weight of all our responsibilities.

Our intensities.

Our stone-faced seriousness.

Our stresses that have us so tired.

Our dreams that have us so frantic.

The cross was pounded into the ground that day for our release.

If only we remember what has already been done for us.

If only we learn to lay down the load.

———

I pray the day will come when women everywhere, so burdened with so much, will come home to the Cross and know joy again, that the load might shift from their shoulders to God's.

I pray the day will come when women everywhere can be so at home with themselves they will be able to whistle and smile and sing again, even while they work.

I pray for our sake that day will come soon.

For Thought, Journaling, or Discussion:

1. Do you see any reasons why women might be more intense today than they were fifty years ago?
2. In what ways have new opportunities for women also created new burdens for them?
3. What suggestions would you have for the woman who says she has no joy in her life anymore because of all her heavy responsibilities?
4. You may have heard it said, "Laughter is the best medicine." What might laughter be able to do for you?
5. Do you often forget to laugh? If so, why do you suppose that is?
6. How have your intensities gotten in the way for you?
7. How have your disappointments gotten in the way?
8. Read Isaiah 61:1–3, which is a prediction of Jesus' coming mission to earth. What does the passage have to do with joy? In what ways did Jesus seek to return "lightheartedness" to people?
9. In what ways do you need to return "lightheartedness" to your life? In what ways do you need to relearn joy? What are some steps you might take to do so?
10. Trace the word "joy" through Scripture. List ten conclusions you come to about joy.

FIVE

....

Even our compassionate side has fallen on hard times these days. We're not sure we like the label "caregiver" anymore.

....

Real Women Don't Cry

Emotional Sensitivities

It is February of a national election year, time for the New Hampshire primary. The morning newspaper describes the New Hampshire primary as "an institution now imbedded in the history, and the folklore, of the entire country."

But that isn't what catches my eye this morning as I glance at the front-page article. What catches my eye is the picture of a snow-covered presidential candidate standing on a platform, microphone in hand, addressing a crowd who had obviously braved the elements with him. The caption under the picture reads: "Whether he shed tears or not, the perception that Senator Ed Muskie cried in the 1972 New Hampshire campaign wounded his chances for the nomination."

But that campaign was years ago. Today, we have laid aside the assumption that real men don't cry. Surely today, in a more "enlightened" time, we would allow presidential candidates to cry in public if the occasion seemed appropriate.

Or would we?

And an even more interesting question: Would we allow that candidate to cry were she a woman?

I don't think we would. I don't think women are even allowing themselves to cry these days. Maybe we feel that to compete in a male-dominated market we've got to stifle our tears, toughen up, put on our armor of steel. Maybe we feel that the day of the emotional female is past, and now we've got to learn to operate out of our head, not from our heart.

Unfortunately, as we operate more and more out of our head and less and less from our heart, the day of our intuitive strengths—as well as some other significant assets—may also be fading.

Maybe we *have* been too controlled by our emotions at times. Maybe we have not always used our reasoning power to its fullest. In fact, I daresay, it is true we have not. And yes, it is high time we wake up to our cognitive selves. There is never an excuse for short-cutting our brain.

However great the danger of under-using our brain, equally great is the danger of using it to the exclusion of our heart. Nothing wrong with shoring up our brain power—as long as we leave our heart intact. Once we go to meddling with our heart, we women stand to lose a great deal.

We stand to lose our tears.

For years I wore contact lenses, and I know, medically speaking, there is nothing worse than dry eyes. *Emotionally* speaking, there is nothing worse than dry eyes.

But we haven't quite caught on to that yet. How many times have you told yourself: *Buck up, old gal. Don't let them see you cry.*

If the general population would not tolerate the late Senator Ed Muskie's tears in 1972, I wonder how much less tolerant they are today of your tears or mine. Sad is the day when women cannot cry simply because we may have cried too much in the past.

Remember how soothing it can be to cry? Not manipulative, artificial tears. Those go with games children play. But genuine, from the bottom of your soul, bottom of your feet, bottom of your despair kind of tears. Tears that speak a thousand words without having to utter one.

I once filled a whole afternoon and evening with my tears—grieving tears, at having to move from a community, a house, and people I dearly loved. The tears started to flow about two in the afternoon and they didn't subside until after ten that night. But when all the crying had ended, I slept better than I'd slept in months. My tears had been my comfort. They'd washed over my grief and led me to a new dimension. After that, I began to actually anticipate the move.

Jesus was "person" enough to cry. And in public at that. He stopped his entourage in the middle of the road to Jerusalem, looked down on the city he loved—a city so wrapped in itself that it had no time for him—and gave room for his tears of disappointment to flow (Luke 19:41).

But what will the disciples think?

Apparently it didn't matter to Jesus.

And what about the crowd gathered to mourn Lazarus? Certainly, everyone cries at a funeral. But not Jesus, this one traveling the country claiming to be the Messiah. Certainly, if he was God, he would be above tears.

He was God, but he was not above tears.

He stepped right up into the focal point of the action and stood there by Lazarus' grave and wept openly, unashamedly (John 11). No stifling of tears for the Son of God. He had nothing to prove, nothing to lose. He let his tears run their natural course.

Oh, that our lives would be so authentic.

———————

After forty years, I still remember many things about Abbie Gail Ashcraft—a grand old woman of the South where I lived. I remember what a wise woman she was, and so gentle and loving. I remember her big white house with blue shutters. I remember having tea in her living room, drinking from her pretty bone china teacups. I remember how much of a lady I felt when I went to visit her with my mother.

I remember how everyone looked up to Abbie Gail. She had Bible studies in her living room and played the organ for the large church just down the street from her house. The minister of her church (who was also a good friend of my father) often talked about Abbie Gail and how he depended on her for many things, even though she was almost old enough to be his grandmother.

But what I remember most are her tears—the ones that often misted in her eyes when she talked about things that meant a lot to her. And interestingly enough, her tears always seemed to be tears of delight—even though Abbie Gail also had reason for tears of sadness, I'd been told. It seems, according to the legend, her fiancé had been killed in the war and she had never married because of her broken heart.

Many years have passed since I knew Abbie Gail. But the

impression has not. Abbie Gail was strong. But she also often got tears in her eyes. The message I received as a ten-year-old was this: The strong also cry. In fact, maybe they are strong because they cry.

It is a message women need to hear today.

Sad is the day when we dam up our tears for fear we will damage the cause of womanhood.

Even sadder the day we cannot be sentimental anymore— just because we are women; when we have to give up senti- mentality for the sake of our more "thoughtful" image. As though sentiment and thought cannot exist in the same body.

My mother is still sentimental—I mean downright, mushy sentimental—the kind of sentimental that was scripted all over the valentine she sent me this week. (Valentine's Day was yesterday.)

And my mother was mushy about my dad on Valentine's Day too. She is, in fact, always mushy about my dad. But I'm not too concerned. I have never seen a marriage die because of too much mush. I *have* seen marriages die from not enough of it. Over the phone, on a long-distance phone rate, she read me every word on the valentine card Daddy gave her (and it was one of those three-pager cards). Plus, she went into a de- tailed description of the long-stemmed red roses he sent, right down to great-grandma's antique vase she put them in.

No doubt about it: My mother is a sentimentalist.

I admire her for it. I think her life is fuller because of it. I think my life is fuller because of it. And I do not think it has detracted from her ability to think and reason. Maybe her thoughts are even more insightful because they are coupled with sentiment.

I am not my mother. I am a different creature, of a different style, in a different world. To wear a brand of sentimentality that does not fit me would be a great waste. But to wear no sentimentality at all would also be a great waste.

It would be a great waste for my loved ones. Some of them claim they do not like to "be slobbered over," and yet when they receive no "slobbering over" at all, they are the first to cry foul. Something is wrong, they think, with a mother who does not mush.

Even the most stoic among our loved ones—the ones who claim to need no fussing over—probably need to be fussed over the most. They need the nourishment it brings, the message it sends: You are wonderful and I love you very, very, very much.

Strip ourselves of sentimentality, and those we love are sure to suffer.

Strip ourselves of sentimentality, and we are sure to suffer.

Some would argue just the opposite. Some would say: Teach yourself not to feel and you will never be hurt again. They may be partially right. Short-term, you may not feel the pain. But the long-term picture is something quite different. Turn off your feelings, and you do not feel the pain. But turn off your feelings and you've also blocked out pleasure. A life without pleasure or pain would make one little more than the chair she sits on.

Pleasure is not a foreign concept with God. Scripture is full of references to it. God takes delight in his people (Psalm 149:4). God delights in me (Zephaniah 3:17). The authors of Scripture, it seems, were always delighting in something. They lifted up their eyes to the hills. They walked by still waters. They considered the heavens. They danced in the temple. They pored over God's commands with joy. (The Book of

Psalms.) As though that's not enough, an entire book of the Bible is given over to the celebration of physical pleasure (Song of Solomon). I cannot conceive that God would have created us with such a great capacity to feel pleasure and then said, "Now, don't you dare feel it—especially if you are a woman and you want to be taken seriously!"

For all the celebrations of pleasure recorded in the Bible, there are equal references to pain. God does not sit in his celestial powerhouse sending out bolts of affliction because he wants us to know pain. Yet once pain knocks, he does want us to open the door to it. He wants the pain to season us, to mellow us, to scrounge around and do its work in us. Pain has a work to do in us, just as pleasure does (James 1). Both are part of God's plan. So when I no longer allow myself to feel I am actually thwarting his plan.

We must keep feeling, for the sake of allowing pain and pleasure to do their work.

We must keep feeling, for the sake of keeping our five senses alive.

Today, two things work against our senses: time and technology. Women simply do not have time anymore to sit around noticing whatever it is they are touching, tasting, hearing, seeing, smelling. Instead, our fingers fly over keyboards and we gulp down coffee on the run.

I am sad about that.

I am sad that I do not always taste my coffee when I drink it. I don't taste it because my mind is occupied with the events of the day to come. And what a waste of the rich, deep, hazelnut flavor that fills my kitchen every morning.

We live in a college town—not far from the college chapel. The carillons chime every quarter hour. At six in the evening they play vespers. How tragic that I cannot tell you what they played last night, or the night before that, or the night before that. I was busy at my computer while the chimes were ringing.

The press of business has a way of dulling our senses. And sometimes the more business we take on, the duller our senses become.

Too much analysis can dull the senses.

Used to be, I sat in the sun and luxuriated in the feeling of warmth on my skin. Now when I sit in the sun, all I can think of is how many units of radiation I'm taking into my skin and how long it will be before I have to start chemotherapy for skin cancer. Used to be, I walked to the park and noticed every bird along the way. Now I walk to the park and calculate how many calories I'm burning up.

I'm glad women today are more conscious of their health. I'm glad we count calories and worry about skin cancer. We are smarter to do it. But I wonder too if too much of a good thing can come full circle and become too much of a dangerous thing. If we are so analytical about every move we make and its effect on our health, we might not die of skin cancer or obesity, but we may well drop of a heart attack from all our worrying.

And then too: When our senses are dulled, think of all the beauty around us we miss.

I have on occasion wondered how God must feel about all my overlooking of the work of art he has created for my enjoyment. Maybe he feels a little like an artist who has labored long and lovingly over his masterpiece—and then no one shows up for his exhibit.

I need to keep my senses fine-tuned, if for no other reason than this: to keep appreciating the beauty, yes—but most of all, to appreciate its Creator. I especially need to remember who's behind it all because, forceful person that I am, I sometimes imagine I'm in charge. Nature gives me perspective on myself as well as on God.

"When I consider your heavens, the work of your fingers, the moon and the stars, which you have set in place, what is man that you are mindful of him, the son of man that you care for him?" (Psalm 8:3–4).

My emotions are a conduit to wonder—the wonder of God's care and love for me.

My emotions lead me to love and care for others as God has loved and cared for me.

Women are good at caring, "they" say. For the most part, "they" are right. We always have been empathic—some of us better at it than others. We often feel another's pain, even before the pain's been expressed. It is our intuitive side at work. It grows out of our compassion. But even our compassionate side has fallen on hard times these days. We're not sure we like the label "caregiver" anymore. We're not certain we have the time or energy to be all that compassionate anymore.

True, compassion can lead to all sorts of entanglements. You *do* spend enormous amounts of time and energy on other people. You connect with them. They walk into your heart without knocking. Sometimes they get into your heart and you wish they weren't there.

Sometimes we wish we were machines, because that way we wouldn't have to get involved.

But is that what we really want?

Do we really want to dump intuition and compassion and all the warmth that goes with it? If we cut off emotion, all of this goes.

Where would our relationships be if we were to unplug our feelings?

Our friendships might limp along. We are probably smart enough to pull off relationships by pure intellect. Our bookshelves are filled with the theory. So even without the emotional attachment, we *could* apply the how-to's, and *voila!* Instant friendship.

But not sustaining friendship.

Friendship is maintained not by skill but by our ability to feel with each other.

————

I read between the lines of my adult daughter's letter. And I know she is frightened about the future. Where will she and her husband be a year from now? Will he find a job now that his seven years of education are finished? Will they be able to conceive a child? Afford a house? Many questions. Few answers.

If I did not allow myself to feel so deeply, I would simply point out the high statistical probability of her husband's finding a job, of their buying a house, of conceiving a child. Or I would suggest a book to read or a seminar to attend.

But this is not what my daughter wants. It is not what she needs.

She tells me her fears again when I call her.

And then we come together as only mother and daughter can—drawn by uncertainty. She hops in her car and comes the three hundred miles to me.

She comes with her pain. But her pain is in my heart too.

It is pain that keeps us coming together. Keeps us depending upon each other. Keeps us reading between the lines so we are sure not to miss anything with each other.

Where would mothers and daughters be if they couldn't feel with each other?

Where would any of us be?

We would be just this side of technology.

We would be our computers.

We would be polite formalities. *Hi. How are you. But please don't tell me.*

We would be all schedule. We would sit across the table from someone at lunch and wonder: *When will she ever stop talking so I can get on with important things?*

We would be babbling talk, with no connection to anyone's heart.

We would be the roll of distant thunder. Noise on the horizon. But always distant. *Always* distant. Never coming closer. We would hold people at arm's length.

I wonder if that is really what we want?

I think not.

I think we want closeness.

I think we want to stay fully human—to keep our *heart* and our *head* in balance. We know one is not more female than the other. One is not more male. We do not go solely for the heart or the head at the expense of the other. We go for both.

We use our reason, but we do not apologize for our emotion. Nor do we allow another to discredit us because of our feelings.

———

Don't give me that crying stuff again!

We let the tears come, but we use our head to respond: "I am crying because I am hurt. You are rejecting me when you reject my tears."

We make sure we are not playing games with our emotions or manipulating someone into doing what we want them to do. Pouting and whining and withholding favor as a form of punishment is unacceptable. We honestly state how we are feeling. To do this, we have to stay alert to how we are feeling. Sometimes talking with someone tells us how we are feeling. Sometimes writing. Or praying. Or reading Scripture.

"My God, my God, why have you forsaken me?" (Mark 15:34).

With Jesus, we name our despair. We have felt rejection's sting too.

We admit it to ourselves. We admit it to each other. And once our feelings are admitted, we do not wallow in self-pity or seek sympathy. We simply tell what we feel so others can better understand us, so we can better understand ourselves. It is the coming together of our emotions and our intellect. We acknowledge feelings so we can understand. Emotions and intellect serve each other.

And we continue to trust our emotions, as the good friends that they are.

Sometimes good friends let us down. Or they are unreliable. But we don't throw them overboard. Rather, we say, "Oh, I see something has gone wrong here. Let's see what it is." But then, "Let's pick up and go on."

When our heart leads us down some forbidden lane where our head would not have led, we acknowledge it with humility. We have learned our lesson well. The lesson is this: There will be a tomorrow. And tomorrow always comes with the consequences of today. So before I follow my heart again (without taking along my head), I will ask myself, *Where is this leading me? Who might this be harming? How will I feel about all this ten years from now?*

When emotions cut themselves loose from responsible reason, we must muster all the cognitive resources within us to haul our emotions back into line. We must reason with ourselves. We must open our minds to God so he can reason with us.

" 'Come now, let us reason together,' says the Lord. 'Though your sins are like scarlet, they shall be as white as snow; though they are red as crimson, they shall be like wool' " (Isaiah 1:18).

In the end, it is God's grace that reels us back in. But it is also our minds. We probably do not *feel* like being hauled back in. But we *know* it is best. And we give thanks for God's grace and protection. We also thank him for the mental resources he has given that have come to our aid.

Then we decide: *Next time I will be more careful about turning my emotions loose without using my brain to keep them in check.*

Once again, our reason and our emotion work together, keeping us in balance.

Reason and emotion. One is not more important than the other. Both will service us well, as long as we give permission to each.

So. Who's to say real women don't cry anymore?

We've just begun to realize the power of a strong head *and* a strong heart.

For Thought, Journaling, or Discussion:

1. In your opinion, are women innately more emotional than men—or is the difference cultural?
2. Do you think women today seem to fear their emotions? If so, why do you think this is true?
3. What do you think is the greater danger women face today: feeling too much or feeling too little? Give reasons for your answer.
4. What is the balance between stoicism and unhealthy sentimentality? How does one find it?
5. On a scale of zero to ten, with ten being highly emotional and zero being very unemotional, where would you rate yourself?
6. Are you comfortable with where you appear on the scale?
7. If not, what would you like to see change?
8. Finish this sentence: When it comes to the balance between emotion and reason, a woman is in balance if ___.
9. What biblical principles apply in regard to how we handle our feelings?
10. What biblical principles apply in regard to how we handle our reason—our intellect?

SIX

················

I am sad that women today live in such isolation from one another. Perhaps we are paying a price for our newfound strength.

················

Hiking Solo Up the Mountain

Our Need for Each Other

"Free to be, you and me."

The slogan got a lot of press a number of years ago. And women have in some ways taken it to heart. We've been trying for a long time to distinguish ourselves from one another. We are more than someone's wife, mother, daughter, friend. We're ourselves. We're separate. Independent. One of a kind. A stand-alone, if you will.

Our reasoning was this: It's high time we cut the umbilical cord and became ourselves. We no longer settle for being attached at the hip to anyone. We have our own brain now. Our own bank account. Many of us marry and keep our maiden name. All for the sake of our identity. We were born to be who we are. Why complicate it through self-obliterating alliances in which we forget who we were meant to be? Or become so engrossed in another's life that we actually take on their persona?

Finally, we are getting around to being ourselves.

Finally, we have found ourselves.

But . . .

Having found ourselves, we may have lost something in the process—like connectedness with other women.

How did this unfortunate saga unfold?

Here's one possibility:

Once upon a time, we perceived ourselves as weak. And we wanted to be strong. We saw our weakness due in part to the fact that we were somebody's shadow—primarily our husbands. Shadows have no power in themselves. They simply follow the moves of the main player. Nor do they have any life outside the life of their counterpart. They are somebody else's reflected glory.

How sad to be only a shadow, we thought to ourselves. *We must do something about this helpless state of affairs.*

So we determined to make ourselves into something more than shadows. We took on a separateness. A distinction. We want to *stand* on our own. We wanted to stand *out* on our own. Our strength carried us to a new day of independence not only from husbands, but from everyone. Now we could celebrate the Fourth of July all year long. Happy to say, we didn't really *need* anyone anymore. We had self-sufficiency firmly by the hand.

And that gave us a new confidence. We knew the way on

our own now. We didn't need another to take us by the hand.

I consider myself a self-starter. I consider myself a head-starter. I remember cutting a path up a North Carolina mountainside where our family was hiking. It seemed to me that my way was a faster way to the top of the mountain. So I simply struck off in the lead, assuming everyone would follow.

But my followers didn't follow. They had their own ideas about getting to the top of the mountain. And they started off another way. Several moments of panic at the thought of being alone on those mountains were enough to send me scurrying back down the path in search of the others. It was much more comforting to hike to the top of the mountain with the other members of my family.

The danger of being a self-starter, a head-starter, is that you may lose yourself from the rest of the group and no longer have the comfort of their company.

Seems to be where a lot of women are today—doing the mountain solo, cut off from other women who could offer support and companionship. We know the way now, so we've struck off on our own.

Or maybe we choose to stay with the pack, but the very last thing we want to do is fall in line behind another woman. We will stay with the group as long as we can *lead* the group. If we can't be at the head, forget the group. Back to doing our own thing. That way we are the leader, the follower, and everything in between. We *are* the group. Such a sorry, solitary group of one we are.

I am sad that women today live in such isolation from one another. Perhaps we are paying a price for our newfound strength.

Our strength can work *for* us. Strength makes us able to offer things of significance to someone else—gifts that have matured and developed because of our courage and confidence.

But our strength can also work *against* us. Strength takes away our motivation to form associations. When a woman is strong, she can be a self-contained unit and still survive. Not only survive, but thrive.

True, we have not always formed associations for the healthiest of reasons. Sometimes we have not felt valuable on our own. So we have formed alliances we hoped would give us value. Or we felt life was boring and linked up with another because we needed excitement.

Or maybe we wanted to know how to do something another person knew how to do, and we thought hanging out with that person would cause some secret formula to pop forth.

Or maybe we looked at someone's life and said, "That's the kind of life I want for myself." So we got close to that person in hope the magic would rub off.

But today, women don't have to live vicariously anymore. (Except maybe in romance novels.) Now that we have opportunity, we can say, "That's the kind of life I want for myself and *I* will make it happen."

And we *do* make it happen. So we don't need our associations anymore to make up for what we lack. (It is, in many ways, a step in the right direction.) But how that sometimes translates is: We don't need our associations anymore. Period.

Another thing: With our reentry into the workplace, we've tasted control and we like the taste. Sweet as honey to our lips. The last thing we are looking for is opportunity to give control away. But we know that every time we form a friendship, we relinquish a piece of our control. (It is what Christian relationships of any kind are all about.) So we are thinking twice these days about deep commitments to friendships. We are not so sure we want to have to swallow our pride, as everyone in a friendship (or a marriage) has to do at one time or another, and say, "Your way makes more sense. We will do it your way." But sometimes that is exactly what a friendship (or a marriage) calls for.

Relinquishment. It sets the sirens screaming in our brain. We relinquished once and look where it got us. Please don't expect us to relinquish again. It is a price too high to ask, even for the sake of friendships. So we continue to hold tightly to ourselves, forgetting that Jesus came to give himself away and that we are to follow in his steps.

Control isn't the only thing we have to share when we connect with each other. We have to share our time.

We protect our time with our lives. And we never, ever seem to have enough of it. But I wonder: Could it be that our zeal for controlling our time has eaten us up—or at least eaten up our friendships? That we have become so well-managed that we can't squeeze each other in anymore?

Time isn't so easily guarded in relationships. There is an ambiguity to friendship. You cannot predict how much time it will take. Or when you might be called on to hand over some of your carefully managed moments.

I think of a word when it comes to this matter of women being connected to other women—a word I learned in biology. The word is "symbiotic." It means "the living together in close union of two dissimilar organisms, in a mutually beneficial relationship."

I think of a story that goes with the word "symbiotic." It is a biblical story of two very dissimilar women who came together in a mutually beneficial relationship.

Ruth and Naomi had one thing in common—they'd both lost husbands. But there the similarities ended. Naomi was Jewish. Ruth, a Moabite. (Israel and Moab didn't mix very well as a rule.) Naomi was from Bethlehem; Ruth from across the state line. Naomi's people worshiped Jehovah God. Ruth's people bowed to the deity Chemosh. The Jews spoke one form of Hebrew, the Moabites, another. Ruth was young. Naomi, older. Naomi had had children. Ruth had none.

But the two women connected. And not simply because they were linked through marriage. Ruth's husband had died. She could have chosen to let the relationship with her mother-in-law die too, especially when Naomi said, "I think I'll pack my bags and head back over the hills toward home."

Talk about connectedness. Ruth packed her bags and followed Naomi home. Once settled in Bethlehem, Ruth went off to the barley fields to gather the day's meal. (Barley fields were probably much too hot a place for a woman Naomi's age.) Talk about a "mutually beneficial relationship." Ruth happened to end up in the very field owned by one of Naomi's relatives— the very relative who happened to be "next of kin" to Naomi, the one who ended up becoming Ruth's husband.

From a purely human point of view, there was something wrong with this picture—Ruth marrying Naomi's relative Boaz. Naomi was closer to his age than Ruth was. Naomi, not Ruth, was the Jewish woman who was protected by the law of the "kinsman-redeemer." And I imagine Naomi, even in her old age, would have liked to have had another husband too. She probably didn't like going to bed with no one to put her cold feet against any more than Ruth did. *Naomi and Boaz.* That's how the marriage certificate *should* have read.

And that's how the marriage certificate *would* have read,

except for the connectedness of these two women. For when you are truly joined in spirit, another woman's good is your good too. You work for the good of each other.

But, you say, in this case, it looks like Ruth got all the goods.

Not really. Yes, she got the husband, Boaz. And she got a son, Obed. But Naomi benefited too. One morning at the well, some women of the town said to her, "Praise be to the Lord, who this day has not left you without a kinsman-redeemer. May he become famous throughout Israel! He will renew your life and sustain you in your old age. For your daughter-in-law, who loves you and who is better to you than seven sons, has given him birth" (Ruth 4:14–15).

The happy ending to the story is this:

"Then Naomi took the child, laid him in her lap and cared for him. The women living there said, 'Naomi has a son.' And they named him Obed. He was the father of Jesse, the father of David" (Ruth 4:16–17).

We know the postscript to the story. From David's family tree came Jesus, the Messiah, the only begotten Son of God.

Perhaps it's time we reconsider the benefits of staying connected. Perhaps it's time we rethink our level of commitment to each other, willingly surrendering some of our carefully guarded control, our well-managed moments.

———

Why do we need to stay connected with other women?

It is fantasy to believe we will always be strong. Even the strongest among us will someday face something that will cause us to wilt like a daisy in the sun. Sooner or later, something will drain the self-assuredness right out of our veins.

What then?

Who will be there for us then?

Oh yes, family will be there. But when pain runs in my blood, it runs in the blood of all my family. Who will be there as a friend, caring deeply for me but separated enough from my pain to look at things realistically? Who will keep a level enough head to point me in the right direction? As an old pop song teaches us, we need each other.

Lean on me
When you're not strong.
I'll be your friend.
I'll help you carry on.
For it won't be long
Till I'm going to need
Somebody to lean on.

It's what connectedness is all about—somebody to lean on.

————

Connectedness is also having somebody to learn from.

We know a lot these days. But the smartest people in the world are the ones who readily admit they don't know it all. With all our opportunities for learning today, women should be like dry fields taking in the summer rains. We should be soaking it up.

And we *are*. We are good at soaking it up—to a certain extent. We are good at learning from books. It is a sign of our intellectual curiosity. Or learning from men. (Sometimes our old biases still show through.) But sometimes we are not so good at learning from other women. To sit at the feet of a woman who is our peer? Well, that seems to be another matter.

Why is that?

I can only guess.

Maybe we have lapsed back into competing with one another. Maybe learning from another woman is an open admission that she knows something I don't. Maybe that is a bitter pill for us to swallow. Maybe we'd rather be the teacher of other women. To be a learner is a lesson in humility we'd rather not have to learn.

We must stay connected for the sake of what we can learn from each other—for the incredible amount of knowledge, wisdom, and information other women can pass on to us.

How fortunate for us when we can learn from each other. We get double value. We get our experiences, plus another's. We get our thoughts, plus someone else's. We get what we have learned through the years *and* what another has learned through the years.

Think how well-informed we *could* be.

Think how in touch with the past we could be if we stayed in touch with each other. We could be the conveyors of memories for each other and for each other's children.

We could say, "Remember when . . ." and then laugh and cry and tell the stories once again for our offspring to hear.

We could go to our bookshelves, pull out the old photo album, and find each other in the pages of our past. We could see changes for the good in each other. We could point out those changes to each other. And be happy together about them. We could look with sorrow at the slopes down which one or the other of us may have slid from time to time. We will not be happy about the slide, but we will be happy that we have stuck by each other even in the decline. There is something comforting about someone knowing your past and loving you anyway. There is something satisfying in knowing that you have stood by someone through all their wanderings.

Sometimes the world is big and wide and scary, even to the most confident of us. There is something secure about someone holding your hand when the crowd is pressing in on you. You are not as likely to be swallowed up or pulled along. Someone will know if you happen to disappear, and they will come looking for you.

Connectedness comforts the child in us.

———

Back in 1936, when my mother graduated from high school, women didn't strike off on their own so much. They still needed each other back then. So my mother and a group of her girlfriends formed a club. They called themselves "The Happy Hearts." That club has gotten together every other month for the last sixty years! Even when my mother was away from them for a number of years in mission work in Alabama, they supported her financially and wrote faithfully. Some of them even took the 1100-mile trip to visit her (and that was before the days of consumer airline travel).

Three of the Happy Hearts have died. But the other eight have carried on valiantly. They are as committed to each other today, my mother says, as they were on the day they first got together.

They are bright spots in one anothers' lives. At the beginning of each year, they pull names to find out who their "secret sister" will be for the year. My mother's house is full of gifts from her secret sisters. Birthdays. Anniversaries. Christmas. Valentine's Day. In sickness and in health. For no apparent reason at all. These eight women are there for each other.

The last time I was home I went with my mother to visit one of the Happy Hearts. Aunt Ruth (I've called her "aunt" all my life) and her husband had just sold their home of fifty years and moved into a retirement center. I was given the grand tour of the new apartment, filled with lifetime memorabilia—some treasures I've been seeing for as long as I can remember. (One thing the Happy Hearts do: They not only connect with one another, they connect with one another's families.)

The highlight of the tour was when Aunt Ruth pulled out her old black photo album. There were my mother and daddy, smiling at me from the pages. Mother and Daddy before I knew them. Mother and Daddy in their courting years, sitting on rocks somewhere up in the mountains, standing beside my dad's 1937 Ford, squinting into the camera with the Atlantic Ocean in the background. Mother and Daddy on their wedding day, Aunt Ruth and her husband standing on either side. With every picture there was a story. I've been hearing the stories for years. I never grow tired of them.

Connections. Sixty-plus years' worth of vital linkage. It is what "The Happy Hearts" are all about. Passing down the stories. Showing the pictures. Telling each other's children and their children's children and their children's children's children.

It is what commitment in friendship is all about.

———

The time has come for us to reconnect. It is time for us to remember each other. To humbly admit how much we need each other. To commit to the details of remembering what is going on in another's life. Important dates. Prayer requests. Tough assignments coming up.

To commit to hanging on to each other so that one or the other of us doesn't slip. And if we notice a slide beginning, to lovingly and gently point to the consequences.

To always be there for each other, never running away in fear or hurt. And if fear or hurt is threatening to break off connections, to mentally take note and say to the other, "I need you. Please. What can we do to fix this?"

It is time we stay connected, no matter what, hanging on to one another the way God patiently hangs on to us.

"For I am convinced that neither death nor life, neither angels nor demons, neither the present nor the future, nor any powers, neither height nor depth, nor anything else in all creation, will be able to separate us from the love of God that is in Christ Jesus our Lord" (Romans 8:38–39).

God forbid we ever become so strong, so independent, so "free" that we let go of other women just at the time we need them so desperately.

———

I have never met Mother Teresa. But I have been in the same room with her. Granted, it was a very large room. And from where I was sitting, I could not really look into her eyes. But I felt she was looking into mine. Her voice was thin, her accent thick. But I don't think I've ever had words impact me more.

Her words were not all that impacted me.

It was a grand meal we were treated to that day. But Mother Teresa was nowhere to be seen while we ate. She did not sit at the head table with the other notables. Afterward I learned she had been down in the basement eating rice with the sisters of her order.

In this day when we are more likely to be off caring for ourselves, caring about ourselves, eating at the "head tables," Mother Teresa's example is not to be overlooked.

She never forgot her sisters.

And she was willing to sit in the basement with them and eat rice rather than feast on the riches of the limelight.

May God grant us the courage to do likewise.

For Thought, Journaling, or Discussion:

1. Do you think some women need associations more than others?

2. How would you respond to the woman who says: "I don't need friendships with other women. My husband is my best friend and he is all I need"?

3. Do you think women need other women more or less today than they did fifty years ago?

4. What are some things that work against women's friendships today?

5. What things could work for them?

6. Why do you think today's woman finds it particularly difficult to give herself to deeply committed friendships?

7. For you, what is it that makes deeply committed friendships with other women most difficult?

8. What makes them work?

9. If you were to follow Jesus' example, what would you do differently in your relationships? Give specific examples of what Jesus did and write down where you found the example in the Bible.

10. If you were to follow Paul's example, what would you do differently in your relationships? Again, give the Bible references for the examples. (Check out especially Galatians, Ephesians, Philippians, Colossians.)

SEVEN

....

*Women today are in such a hurry we never
get around to attaching meaning to the
events of our lives. We never stop to ask
ourselves: What does all this mean?*

....

Hang Up the Dreamin'

The Ability to Reflect

For today's modern woman, there is something rather old-fashioned about the notion of contemplation. We are not very reflective women anymore. We are *do*ers. Because of all our opportunities and all our involvements, we simply don't have time to sit around and be contemplative. It might have worked for women in the 1800s or women who had given themselves to some monastic group, but not for women racing to catch the 7:20 train to the city. Not for women with goals to achieve and schedules to keep.

Where did the process start, I ask myself. *This letting go of our times of quiet and solitude and reflection?*

Here's one possibility: Women feel they have been catching up for a long, long time. It feels like we have always been behind; that we will always be behind. And my guess is that no matter how far along we get, we will always feel as though we have not quite caught up. So we must be forever moving, forever going forward, forever trying to make up for all the time we have lost.

Throw into the mix all we must achieve if we are to stay competitive. We have sharpened our skills. Now we must keep them sharp. We have polished our abilities. It takes a lot of doing to keep them from tarnishing again.

This leads us to live in a state of urgency, like we are always late for something. We cannot possibly afford to sit around in quiet contemplation. We might miss some opportunity. Or the fulfillment of some goal. We must be forever "seizing the moment" or we will miss our chance.

We are much too concrete today to be contemplative. We are women of the bottom line. *What will I have to show for it?* is the thought behind most everything we do. And true, after an hour of sitting quietly, one has little she can hold in her hand as evidence of her productivity.

Then too, we feel women have been passive for too long. Contemplation is an act of passivity. We have shifted from passive to active voice. We are comfortable with the image that we are women on the go. We squirm at the thought of women sitting around, quietly reflecting on one thing or the other. Women have done that for generations. Finally, we have put all that behind us.

———

But there is something lost when we let go of quiet contemplation. As women, we lose. But I think too that the world will lose a great deal because of it.

For example, a life without contemplation quickly loses depth. It becomes like a field that is all top-soil—one strong wind and it is all blown away. It is of no long-term use to anyone. Thought, reflection, engaging of the mind—these are all what it takes if we are to have something to say when we open our mouths, if our ideas are to be clear, concise, and well developed, if we are to make a lasting impact on our children, if we are to pass along wise and godly counsel, if we are to make wise and godly choices.

———————

A well-known evangelist once suggested he had three basic sermons he gave a hundred different ways. But as far as he was concerned, the real Bible scholar in their family was his wife.

"She takes time to study and reflect," the evangelist said.

I have met the evangelist's wife. She is my mother's age. I have been in her home. And I know what the evangelist said about his wife is true. Her house is full of books and cozy corners in which to read them. I especially noticed the pile of classics beside her bed. She told me that when her children were young, she always kept her Bible open on the counter in her kitchen so she could pause and savor Scripture in between her child-rearing activities.

The evangelist's wife had a serene way about her. She did not rush about through the day that we spent together. Even her country kitchen with a big fireplace at one end had a serene way about it—as though it were accustomed to having people sit before it, gaze into a roaring fire, and reflect. We walked the grounds of her home and noticed the birds and flowers and trees as we went. Her front porch was full of rocking chairs. Here was the kind of place you could sit and think for hours.

As we talked I could tell: Words from the evangelist's wife did not float off the top of her head. Everything she said bore the marks of well-seasoned thought. Her images were vivid, her ideas fresh and well-honed. She used examples from history as cases in point. I didn't get the impression she was handing me someone else's warmed-over tidbits. She was giving me bread straight from the oven. They were her own thoughts, developed over years of quiet with God.

And when we said goodbye, just as the sun was setting over the treetops, I felt I'd been truly fed. I had much to think about as I drove away from her home. I am still thinking about some of her words, years later.

It is what comes from spending time with a person who has depth to her life—a person who still knows the importance of reflection. For when there is depth to a person's life, she will have something substantial to give away to others.

———

I have another concern about women who no longer know how to reflect. I think they also lose the ability to step back and gain perspective—to view the bigger picture, see it from God's point of view.

On one particularly tired and irritating morning of a family vacation out West, we came upon a quiet chapel by the side of the road. The little brown A-frame building was set out in an open space, set back from a magnificent range of mountains—perfect for taking in the panorama of peaks as we sat and reflected, looking out the clear glass window.

Nature had painted the canvas for us. We had but to stop and take it in.

And sit and take it in I did. (While the children and Daddy went exploring the valley.)

I remember the colors of the day—*every* color between the chapel and the hazy peaks far off in the distance. I remember looking up, following the lines of the chapel and then the lines of the mountaintops. Up to the peaks. Up into the clouds. Beyond myself and my little trials of the day—wet sleeping bags from the torrential downpour of the night before. Short tempers from the lack of good solid sleep.

My thoughts went up to God. Up to the God who'd promised peace. "You will keep in perfect peace [her] whose mind is steadfast, because [she] trusts in you" (Isaiah 26:3).

I thought about God's peace. I remembered how much I needed it. (What would a 3,000-mile family camping trip turn into without it?) I thought about the peace God's Son had exhibited when he lived so close to people, and with irritations much bigger than mine.

I reflected back on the peace that had pulled us through before on this trip. Flu bugs. An overheated van. Motion sickness. Rainstorms. Sandstorms. Windstorms. Lightning and thunderstorms. Mosquitoes. Uprooted tent stakes and cold, soggy sleeping bags. God's peace had come to me then. It would not desert me now.

By the time my husband and the children had gotten back from their explorations, my spirits had lifted, my anxious mind quieted. Reflection had gotten my eyes off the things that were bugging me and onto the bigger picture—that God was still a God of peace and he had peace to offer me.

A step back where one can view the bigger picture always helps put things in perspective. It is one of the things women stand to lose if they lose the ability to reflect.

If reflection goes, so do the lessons of the past. Women today are likely to live without ever getting around to attaching meaning to the events of our lives. Do we ever stop to ask ourselves: *What does it all mean?*

I grew up in the South, where front porches were a way of life. No one ever built a house without one. The front porch was probably the most important place in a house—and certainly where most important things—like sitting—took place.

To me, the front porch is symbolic of something missing today. We lack places to sit and watch the world and then attach meaning to the world. Yes, the front porch was where people sat and drank iced tea and talked about how the cotton crop was doing. And I miss all the talking—talking for the sheer pleasure of it. But most of all, I miss the sitting, whether we were talking or not—the sitting and thinking.

I miss front porches because they were spaces to reflect. Especially at night, when the duties of the day were finished. You could sit for hours with no sound except that of the night crickets and the squeak of the porch swing chain in its ceiling hook as you pushed back and forth.

You could see the thousand eyes of a summer night, poking at you through the darkness—lightning bugs, reflecting their miniature worlds. Each in a universe of its own—each with a story of its own.

As a child, you could create the stories; your imagination could soar.

Even in your simple faith, you could say to yourself, "What does all this mean, this wonderfully peaceful, magical night?"

You could answer your own question.

It means my heavenly Father has drawn the shades. But he's up there in his big house somewhere, looking down on me. (He can see through the shades.) And he never goes to bed.

And I would draw all kinds of pictures in my head, about the tiny worlds of the lightning bugs, about God in the darkness. About the night.

For me, the night was not a menacing blackness out there, with all sorts of lurking dangers. Night was a gentle blanket thrown over the world so it could sleep without light in its eyes. I learned to feel safe with the night, even as I sat there in the quietness and listened and looked at the dark.

And sometimes now, as an adult who has lived long enough to know that the darkness at times houses danger, I take myself back to my porch swing. To the days of my innocence and trust. I remember how peaceful the night was when you weren't afraid. How the dark didn't feel dark. How strong God seemed. I remember what it was like to trust. And I ask God to make me a child again.

Reflection keeps memory alive. It dips into scenes of my past and finds what it needs to help me face today. It reminds me what I know about God but have so soon forgotten.

Sometimes I wonder where I'd be today if my mother had not seen to it that I had time to sit and do nothing as a child. If she had not nurtured the reflective side of me, even before my thoughts were very well developed. A child can look. My mother taught me to look.

I wonder where I'd be today without our forays into the woods. Mother and children. Pulling the red wagon loaded with blanket, books, a basket filled with peanut butter crackers and pink lemonade, through the acres of tall, long-needled pine that surrounded our house.

Where would I be if we had not often taken to the woods for quiet time? If we had not noticed the delicate designs of the dogwood and the tiny formations of wood violets? If we had not collected pine cones along the way and made them into all sorts of designs on our blanket? If we had not listened for the flutter of bird wings and learned to identify the chirp that went with them?

Where would I be if we had not sat there on our blanket and listened as Mother read book upon book upon book? If we had not stretched out, flat on our backs, and looked up into the green-needled corridors of pine, into the slivers of blue sky and white clouds? Where would I be today if Mother had not taken the time to make sure I noticed the details of the world and watched for God behind it all?

I wonder: Where will our children be if we don't teach them to sit and look?

They may miss glorious sights.

They may never think to ask: *What does all this say to me about God?*

———

Maybe the woods are an easy place to be contemplative. But who lives in the woods anymore? And who lies under the trees on blankets and peers up into the sky? And who packs a basket with peanut butter crackers and pink lemonade? Life in the late twentieth century isn't that much of a picnic anymore. And even if life were a picnic, many women do not have mothers who would think to take them on one.

True. We must look at the world as it is, not as we wish it were. And we must let yesterday be yesterday and get on with the business of today. It is one concept that has helped women march resolutely into their new day. We have not dragged the past with us.

But there is great danger if we so cut off our yesterdays that we have nothing left to reflect upon. We will not have the lessons from the past: *Here is what I did. Here is what my parents did, my grandparents did. Here is what God did. And here is what I learned from it all.*

It is, no doubt, what God had in mind when he so often stressed to Israel: Keep telling your children what I have done for you. Tell them over and over and over. Tell them what it means. Pass along the lessons of history. Teach your children to reflect upon those lessons.

Reflection provides the layering to our lives. It takes an event of our past—a simple sitting on the front porch and looking at the dark—and attaches meaning to it so that it helps us along in our present. *God is still God, even in the dark. "O Lord . . . even the darkness will not be dark to you"* (Psalm 139:4, 12). *I do not need to be afraid.*

We need to attach more meaning to the events of our lives.

But we are so absorbed in the moment we seldom get beyond it to ask, *What does it all mean?*

We do what the people of Jesus' day did when they took the bread he supplied and ate it and turned to each other and said, "My, wasn't that delicious?" No one thought about the miracle and what it meant (John 6).

And Jesus was grieved. They'd missed his point. They never got beyond the fine texture and delicious taste of the bread.

What does it mean? Jesus asked.

What does *it mean?*

They never thought to ask.

They never sat on their front porches and thought to themselves: *What does it mean, this man producing bread for 5,000 when he started with bread enough for only one or two?*

They never took time to write in their journals.

Or if they did write in their journals, they never got around to reflecting. Instead, they wrote the facts—things like:

Today we were out south of town at the hillside arena, attending a special guest lectureship. (Very warm day—82 degrees.) Anyhow, I found the lecturer and what he had to say quite fascinating. But then after sitting so long, I was ready for a coffee break (though actually it was lunchtime by then). But the committee forgot to plan for a coffee break. So the guest lecturer came to the committee's rescue and starting handing out cinnamon rolls. The rolls just kept coming. (He started with five.) In the end, I didn't see anyone who wasn't eating (and there were about 5,000 of us in attendance). It was pretty amazing. The cinnamon rolls were the best I've ever eaten (and I was starved). I had three in all! They had vanilla frosting on top. I think that's what made them so good. And of course they were made with plenty of cinnamon and butter. They were very filling. I didn't even have to eat dinner tonight. If ever I see the lecturer again, I'm going to ask him for his recipe.

They missed the point! They never even *looked* for the point. They never got around to asking: What does this miracle mean?

It is what happens when we never take time for reflection. Life without reflection means we go from one meal to the next, filling our stomachs, yes, but never drawing the nutrients from the food—nutrients vital to our growth.

If the world needs anything today, it needs women who reflect and give careful thought. Thought to their world. Thought to their faith. Thought to the events of their day. Thought to the consequences of their actions. Thought to their past and their future, not just the present.

But thinking takes time. And like everything else, there will be no time for it unless we plan time for it. Living just happens. Reflection is intentional. And the woman who will be a cut above the rest in her faith is the woman who has decided: There *will be* time for reflection in my life—for the study of the Bible, for thought and prayer.

Quiet in itself will not do much for us—except slow down our heartbeat. Sitting and staring out the window will not necessarily make us women of character and conviction. Nor will sitting and repeating words to ourselves. In fact, sitting and staring out the window may allow emotional and spiritual arthritis to set in. Or it may open us up to all sorts of unwanted ideas. But directed quiet—quiet that opens itself to the Word of God and the voice of God—is the kind of quiet that can nourish us.

Godly reflection calls for focus on the right thing—or rather, the right Person.

———

Several years ago, I was sitting quietly on a train, going from Geissen, West Germany, to Amsterdam. I had eight minutes to make a connection in Cologne. Needless to say, I was somewhat concerned about finding the right train for Amsterdam in just eight minutes. To help relieve my anxiety, my friends in Geissen gave me a train schedule. The trouble was, the train schedule was all in German.

As we neared Cologne, my concern mounted. I still did not know which track my next train left from. I continued to search the schedule.

The train began to slow. Time was running out. I thought of one more place to look—at the back of the book. Suddenly I was vaguely aware we were passing by something enormous. I caught only a fleeting glimpse of the majestic 424-foot Cologne Cathedral tower before we pulled into the station.

People drive for hours just to view the impressive structure. I had my sights on the wrong thing!

Israel reflected. But for much of their history, they were reflecting on the wrong thing. Mostly they were reflecting on themselves and the things they had made for themselves. God tried the wake-up call more than once. "See, I am doing a new thing! Now it springs up, [Israel]. Do you not perceive it?" (Isaiah 43:19).

Unfortunately, Israel did not see what God was doing. They were too busy to notice. And it was just a matter of time before Assyria and Babylon marched in and carried the nation off in pieces.

Israel forgot to look.

Looking calls for waiting. Waiting for God.

Interestingly enough, Israel once knew what waiting for God meant.

I'm sure if I had been in the crowd that was skipping out of Egypt that day, I would not have wanted to wait around at the water's edge till Moses finally gave the signal. Especially with Pharaoh's army in hot pursuit.

Whatever is Moses waiting for?

Push ahead.

The Egyptians are coming!!

Had it been me in that crowd, I'd have been shoving on through. But God had a better plan. And it was *wait*.

"Stand firm and you will see the deliverance the Lord will bring you today . . . you need only to be still" (Exodus 14:13–14).

Israel stood still. They waited for God. And they walked

through the sea on dry ground. Not one of them drowned in panic.

Perhaps if we learned to stand still we would see more deliverance.

Perhaps things would be different for us if we did what Jesus told Peter, James, and John to do: "Watch and pray so that you will not fall into temptation" (Mark 14:38).

Perhaps we would be women "after God's own heart" if we did what David did.

David had plenty to do. He was the new king. The prophet Nathan had just brought the word. God had rejected King Saul. David now held the scepter. It was not the time to sit.

But David, in all his wisdom, sat anyhow. He sat before the Lord (2 Samuel 7:18).

At the most critical time of his life, he sat.

Before going into one of the most critical battles of his life, he sat.

And when it came time to get on with the business of being king, he didn't do it perfectly, but he did capture God's heart in the process. And when it was time to go up to battle against the Philistines, he soundly defeated his enemies.

The secret was in the waiting.

The secret is always in the wait.

In the silence.

The listening.

The learning.

The reflecting.

The asking: What does this mean?

"They that wait upon the Lord shall renew their strength" (Isaiah 40:31, KJV).

Our strength will only be as good as our ability to sit patiently and wait.

But we aren't very patient anymore.

We have been conditioned not to be patient. With convenience stores on every other block, we don't have to be patient at all. We can have what we want and we can have it NOW. Maybe people could be patient long ago, when cars didn't go 110 miles an hour and rice didn't cook in four minutes and all kinds of money wasn't available in twenty seconds with the push of a green button at the cash machine. But things are different today and we don't have time to be all that patient.

But I think convenience is selling us short. It is giving us temporary fixes. It is not equipping us for the long haul. The long haul calls for patience. (Just ask any eighty-year-old you know.)

I am all for convenience. I use cash machines and four-minute rice and the corner quickmart. But it is all the more reason I need to learn the art of reflection. I need to learn to slow myself down. I need to think about the long haul and consequences. I need the things reflection can teach me.

I need reflection to take my thoughts deeper. To make me a woman of quality. I cannot grab a spiritual nugget here and there and expect my faith to have substance. Panning for gold means down on your knees, sifting the waters, scrutinizing the gravel, sieveful by sieveful.

Reflection is hard work. It calls for patience in a mostly impatient world. It calls for me to go against my natural grain of running, running, running. It calls for me to reverse my thinking: Something may actually be accomplished while merely sitting.

Maybe *everything* is accomplished while merely sitting— everything of substance, that is.

Maybe if we sat more often, we would speak and act with greater conviction. Maybe we would be women of conviction.

Not women who are going about, always causing a stir because their convictions are clashing with someone else's. But women who know what they believe and why. Women who can always give a reason for the hope that they have (1 Peter 3:15).

Maybe if we sat more often, we would carry around more gentle ways. Maybe we would stay quiet long enough to soak in the flavor of Christ—like meat marinating on the stove. The flavor would have time to seep deep inside us. And then when the crises hit—or even the minor irritations—our natural inclinations that come spilling out would carry the fragrance of Christ (2 Corinthians 2:14).

It is a known fact that when you hang around something long enough, you go home smelling like that something. In high school, I packed hot dogs in my grandfather's meat-packing plant. After eight hours in the packing cooler, I went home with every inch of me smelling like a hot dog. The first thing I did when I got home was to wash the hot dog out of my hair.

It was the absorption factor. Spend time in the presence of hot dogs and you begin to smell like one.

Maybe the same would be true if we spent more time sitting in quiet contemplation, reflecting on God. Certainly, traces of him would show up on our faces, in our words and ways. Maybe our words would not be wrong so often. Maybe they would not wound as much. Maybe they would not be sharp enough to wound. Maybe we would not be so opinionated—so unduly impressed with our own position on a matter. Maybe there would be more room for grace in our lives if we sat quietly and read our Bibles more—if we focused on and prayed to the Master of all grace himself. Maybe the "gentle and humble in heart" that Jesus said of himself (Matthew 11:29) would describe us too.

Maybe, just maybe, strength would flow from us to others if we took time to sit in worship before the Almighty God, Creator of heaven and earth.

Reflection happens in the quiet places. As does worship.

Worship is where we meet God and we pick up our spiritual supplies for the coming day.

Worship is coming into the Holy of Holies.

For Israel, worship took place in the inner sanctum—the Holy of Holies. The priest went into that quiet center by one door, and left by another. (One never leaves the presence of God the same way they came in.) And when the priest came out, he took God's glory to the people. He had been with God in the quiet place. He had something to pass on to the others.

What happens to us in the quiet places cannot help but flow on to others.

It is what Ezekiel sees one day when God's glory returns to the temple at Jerusalem (Ezekiel 47). Ezekiel and a messenger from God are on a walking tour of the temple. At the entrance they stop. Ezekiel takes off his sunglasses, and sure enough, what he thinks he sees is indeed what he sees. A river is flowing out from under the door of the temple, coming from the inner sanctuary.

The angel and Ezekiel follow the river. It flows south and empties into the sea. And here, Ezekiel takes off his sunglasses again. What he thinks he sees is indeed what he sees. When the river merges with the sea, the salt water becomes fresh water and large numbers of fish begin to swim in the waters. More amazing still, wherever the river flows, vegetation springs to life. Fruit trees of all kinds, on both banks of the river, begin to produce. Their leaves never wither and their fruit never fails.

Why?

Says Ezekiel, "Because the water from the sanctuary flows to them. Their fruit will serve for food and their leaves for healing" (v. 12).

It is a picture of what happened when God's glory moved back into the temple at Jerusalem. It is also a picture of what can come from our center of worship—from the quiet times and the quiet places of our lives. Health and healing. To ourselves. To all those we come into contact with along the way.

Reflection for reflection's sake is not enough. Reflection for God's sake is. For it is there we come face-to-face with our loving Creator. The One who made us. And loves us. And wants to share himself with us.

It is what worship is all about.

It is what godly reflection is all about.

And it is what women today so desperately need, in a time where there are so few places to sit and think anymore.

For Thought, Journaling, or Discussion:

1. What indications do you see around you that women may have lost their more reflective side?
2. Why might this have happened?
3. Do you think being contemplative is a personality style, or is it something all women need to develop?
4. Are there any dangers that could come with contemplation? If so, what are they?
5. What biblical support can you give for the notion of quiet reflection and contemplation? Or is it simply a modern idea that has nothing to do with Scripture?
6. How does one keep contemplation from becoming a time for your mind to slip into neutral or to wander?
7. What connection is there between contemplation and private worship?
8. How do you go about making time for quiet with God on a regular basis?
9. What have you found to be the benefits of quiet time alone, especially quiet time alone when you focus exclusively on God?
10. If you haven't been able to develop a pattern of quiet times of reflection and worship, what are some ways you might go about doing it?

EIGHT

....

We have become very good martyrs—quick to let the world know we have been ignored, maligned, and downtrodden. We want the sympathy it evokes. Somehow we feel better about ourselves that way.

....

The Slippery Slope of Women's Rights

Willingness to Surrender

An ad from a weekly news magazine catches my attention today. The ad has a caption in large type that reads: "Lots of ways to be selfish."

It is pushing some IRA money market account, which I don't pay attention to.

But I do pay attention to what the caption says.

It tells me people know what selfishness is all about. It is something we all do so naturally. We are so good at it. And often, it gets us exactly what we want.

Women are paying a lot of attention to themselves these

days. And in many cases, it is for the good. For some of us, it is a new experience. We have ignored ourselves for as long as we can remember. But now we are learning to pay attention to ourselves without getting affixed to ourselves. We care for ourselves so that we can go on to caring for others. We listen to ourselves, but first we listen to God. We stick up for ourselves when it is needed, but we do it with understanding and humility. We make our needs known to another, but first we pray.

Some of us have done that and thus have cared for ourselves without turning self-centered.

Sad to say, some of us have not. Some of us still need permission to care for our legitimate, God-ordained needs. We have yet to understand we are stewards of God's creation, whether that creation is our body or the world around us.

But for all of us, danger is lurking in the shadows—very near to all the attention we are giving ourselves. The danger is that we never get beyond ourselves, that every waking moment we think of ourselves and matters that relate only to us. And even if we do get around to thinking of others, it is about what they can do for us or how we compare to them.

Some of us are old enough to remember LPRs (Long Playing Records). One liability of LPRs was the dust that collected in the grooves and caused the needle to stick. Then you would hear the same note over and over and over until someone pushed the needle ahead.

Maybe we are like a needle stuck in the grove of an old record album. Maybe we are stuck on ourselves. Maybe we are not moving on to the next note, not getting over ourselves.

Maybe we are so stuck on *our* needs that we are no longer sensitive to the needs of people beyond our own little inner circle of close family and friends.

Maybe we are so stuck on our needs that everything we do has this bottom line: *Are my needs being met?*

The trouble with needs is they keep expanding. Like a rubber band, you can stretch them out for a long, long way.

We need what someone else tells us we need. (It is why advertising is such big business.)

We need what another has.

We need what makes us feel good about ourselves.

We need what makes us look better and younger.

We need what will help us relax and be more comfortable.

We need someone who meets our needs.

We need. We need. We need.

Our needs have become our fixation.

And we are drowning in our needs.

We are becoming a self-centered lot.

———

There is an interesting progression to all this attention women are paying to their needs these days. Most often, our needs have not remained simply "our needs." We have decided they are also our rights. And once we decided they were our rights, we began to make demands.

The problem? Once we begin to make demands, we not only lose the attitude of Christ, but we lose our effectiveness. No one wants to listen to demands. Demands never are met very willingly.

So maybe our "demands" have done us in. In the end, we still have not gotten what we wanted or thought we deserved or had a right to.

The progression starts out innocently enough. We are simply "caring for our needs." Nothing wrong with that. But move the "caring for my needs" up one notch to "I deserve this" and we have something else to deal with—our attitude.

The trouble with thinking and talking about our rights is the way we do it—as though the world should be our butler, serving us lunch on a silver tray, not because we are incapable of getting lunch for ourselves but *because we deserve to be served lunch on a silver tray.*

It is an arrogant position. One that others cannot help but notice. One they often choose to resist.

On the other hand, a rather interesting phenomenon sometimes occurs when we stop thinking so much about what we deserve: We end up getting it anyhow. But it comes to us through the back door—the door of surrender.

———

After thirty-two years of marriage, there is one motto I have made mine above all others: *Ruth, give it up.* (And I have to say it over and over and over to myself.)

I do not give it up so I will get it back. (If I do, I have not truly given it up.) But miracle of miracles: When I do truly give it up, I am much more likely to get it back. (This only works when I have no thought whatsoever of coming away with what I had wanted so badly in the first place—such as, *Okay, I give in. Now, since you feel sufficient shame for being so hard-nosed, give it back.* It never works if I think this way. But if I truly put it out of my mind, it often comes back to me as a pleasant surprise.)

Like the perfect lamp I once bought for the antique desk I'd inherited from my grandpa. I had looked and looked for that lamp, and once I saw it I knew it was "The Lamp." Never mind the price tag. I simply handed over the credit card.

What ensued when I got home with the lamp was a rather lengthy (and heated) discussion about spending money we didn't have. Following several days of lobbying on my part, the lamp was causing so much unhappiness in our marriage I took it back to the store. It didn't even matter anymore that it was so perfect for my grandpa's desk.

Christmas was several weeks away. On Christmas morning, a large, mysterious box appeared under the tree. I had completely forgotten about my gained-then-lost treasure until I unwrapped the box and found The Lamp.

It sits on my desk to this day.

No lamp has brought me greater joy, for it was gained through a willingness to surrender.

But surrender is out of vogue these days. Submission has been so demanded of us—held over our heads like a sword. We have not taken to the notion too kindly, because we feel the topic has been beaten to death. And preached from one side only.

I am well aware that some women today *have* been beaten over the head with the rod of surrender. And yes, I know of gross abuses. I have listened to some of the stories. And I am well aware of the theories that are used to support it. But simply because the teaching of submission is abused does not mean it is in itself either unbiblical or emotionally harmful to the point of throwing it out altogether. When one person does all the surrendering or the notion of surrender is used as an excuse for one person to lord it over another (as in a marriage relationship), there is urgent need for counsel. However, when it is used as God intended it—for the benefit of both parties—there is no getting around it.

Oh, but we do look for ways around it. Someone has been unreasonable, un-Christlike, unbiblical in their demand for my surrender. So I will completely ignore the call to submission. Or I will debate what Scripture really says. Or discuss whose place it is to do the giving in. As long as we can debate about it, maybe we won't have to do it.

But according to Scripture, nothing is so Christlike as "giving up." Nothing so freeing as surrender. Nothing that leads to such eternal consequences for both men and women.

It is what Jesus did. (See Philippians 2.)

It is what he calls us to do.

It is at the very heart of the Gospel.

Give up your life so you can find it again.

Lose it so you can keep it.

Of all the people recorded in Scripture who gave up something, not one gave up and lost. They gave up and kept.

Jocabed, the mother of Moses. She put her young son into a flimsy basket and shoved him out into the Nile River one day. It was the ultimate surrender.

"And Moses disappeared among the reeds and was never seen again."

It is not what Scripture says.

Moses was picked up out of that basket by an Egyptian princess and taken to the palace. He went on to become one of the greatest leaders the world has ever seen.

"Since then, no prophet has risen in Israel like Moses, whom the Lord knew face to face, who did all those miraculous signs and wonders the Lord sent him to do in Egypt—to Pharaoh and to all his officials and to his whole land. For no one has ever shown the mighty power or performed the awesome deeds that Moses did in the sight of all Israel" (Deuteronomy 34:10–12).

The poverty-stricken widow of Zarephath. She cleaned out her flour barrel and emptied her oil jug just so the prophet Elijah could have a meal.

"And two weeks later, she and her son were found dead

in their home and the coroner ruled it malnutrition."

Absolutely not.

"There was food every day for Elijah and for the woman and her family. For the jar of flour was not used up and the jug of oil did not run dry, in keeping with the word of the Lord spoken by Elijah" (1 Kings 17:15–16).

The young boy with five loaves of barley bread and two dried salmon. Jesus asked him to give it up.

"And the boy and all that were assembled that day went home hungry. For even Burger King and McDonald's were closed by the time Jesus was finished teaching."

Absolutely not.

"When they had all had enough to eat, he [Jesus] said to his disciples, 'Gather the pieces that are left over. Let nothing be wasted.' So they gathered them and filled twelve baskets with the pieces of the five barley loaves left over by those who had eaten" (John 6:12–13).

God never left his surrendering people empty-handed.

And today, God never leaves those who surrender empty-handed.

Ever.

———

Certainly, God does not leave us high and dry when we surrender.

But others may.

In a perfect world, surrender would always work in our favor. But what about a world where when you give in you are taken advantage of? Or when you give, others take and ask for more? What about a world where there are no checks and balances on abuse?

Jesus once used an interesting image when he sent his disciples out to do door-to-door evangelism. "I am sending you out like sheep among wolves," he said. "Therefore be as shrewd as snakes and as innocent as doves" (Matthew 10:16).

Jesus warned the disciples that they would need to be on guard against the false prophets who would try to take advantage of them while they were witnessing and ministering.

Don't let them get away with it, Jesus seemed to be saying. *Stand up for yourself. But as you stand up, be wise. Don't harm the opposition. Be like gentle sheep among the wolves.*

In fact, Jesus went on to say, "When they arrest you, do not worry about what to say or how to say it. At that time you will be given what to say, for it will not be you speaking, but the Spirit of your Father speaking through you" (vv. 19–20).

In a sense, Jesus was teaching the disciples how to care for themselves—*be gentle, be wise, speak up for yourself but trust me for the words.*

But the "sticking up for themselves" was all in the context of being sent out.

The disciples weren't just sitting around taking care of themselves. They'd already gotten beyond themselves or they would not have been following Jesus in the first place. They'd surrendered all. They'd picked up their sleeping bags and followed him.

True, they forgot from time to time what surrendering their rights was all about—like the time some of them started arguing about the seating arrangement in heaven and who would get the best seats. But Jesus came back with the zinger: *If you want front-row seats, you have to be willing to take the back-seats* (paraphrase of Mark 10:37–38, 43–44).

Forget yourself.

Jesus had to say it over and over to his disciples.

We are just as thick.

He has to say it to us more than once.
Give it up.
Let it go.

————

Jesus spent a great deal of time trying to get people to let go of themselves. A few understood what Jesus was saying and took the risk. Mostly, people loved themselves too much.

Mostly, *we* love ourselves too much.

But if we claim allegiance to Christ, losing ourselves is not an option. It is what Christ requires.

When we are willing to surrender ourselves, we are also willing to surrender whatever it is we think we deserve; whatever we desire; yes, even whatever we own. Sometimes surrender gets very practical. Again, there are lessons to be learned from my mother's generation of women, for I have seen in many of them the ability to hold things (and people, including their children) loosely.

————

For a long time, my mother never had fine china.

Well, that is not exactly true.

She owned it, but she didn't use it.

When she and Daddy packed up and moved to the cotton fields of southern Alabama to start churches in communities where there were no churches, she felt her fine dishes would be inappropriate for her work among people who barely had enough money to grace the table with food, much less fine china. So Mother packed up all her good china (and her mother's china) and stored it in my grandpa's attic. I never even knew she had it until I was almost sixteen and we moved back to the old home area and started unpacking the boxes in Grandpa's attic.

Not only did my mother give up her beautiful things for a while (and she loves beautiful things), she did not play the martyr's role for doing it. I never once heard her talk about the things she'd given up. I didn't grow up feeling sorry for my mother because she'd given up so much for the poor cotton farmers and their families. I don't think it entered my mother's mind to feel sorry for herself. One thing is for sure, she did not try to elicit sympathy from others. Even from her children.

And maybe that is one way of knowing whether or not we have truly surrendered: if we have, we don't feel sorry for ourselves. So we don't feel the need to elicit sympathy from others.

I wonder whether our children will grow up feeling sorry for us. If they do, maybe it's because they've heard nothing but moaning and groaning from us. "Poor me. Poor me. Poor me. Look how bad I have it. Look at all the sacrifices I've been called on to make."

I think it is on this point that women are particularly vulnerable today. We are good martyrs. We are quick to let the world know that we have been ignored, maligned, and downtrodden. We want the sympathy it evokes. Somehow we feel better about ourselves that way.

But it was not the way Jesus took. He didn't need sympathy from anyone. He was not wrapped up in himself. "He was led like a lamb to the slaughter, and as a sheep before her shearers is silent, so he did not open his mouth" (Isaiah 53:7).

Certainly, there is a time to speak. Jesus was not forever

holding his tongue. He had some extremely strong words for people who misrepresented the truth. But when it came to the cup God had given him to drink—the ultimate surrendering of himself—he never once called on the prayer chain to tell people how rotten the Father was treating him.

Several years ago, I spent a few days with the widow of one of the five missionaries who were killed more than thirty years ago by the Auca Indians in Ecuador. The first thing I noticed about the missionary were her eyes. They sparkled. They smiled. She was as natural and carefree as anyone I'd ever met. Certainly as contented and happy.

Never in the two days I was with her did I feel sorry for her. Even when I finally got her to tell me "The Story" once again.

"It is the story God has given me to tell," she said, "even though for a long time, I didn't want to tell it anymore. But God showed me: We all have a story to tell. And this is my story. So I will tell you."

And then her voice got very serious and together we journeyed to the jungle beach where her young husband was speared to death, leaving her with three small children and the prospects of a future alone.

I listened to the story. I felt the tragedy of it all. But I never once felt sorry for the woman who sat across the table from me. She did not feel sorry for herself, so she did not need me to feel sorry for her either. In fact, even though I was there to talk about her, most of the time she wanted to talk about me. I had to keep bringing the conversation back to her.

If ever there was a woman who had moved beyond herself, here was one. She did not demand that her story be told.

Nor did it appear she was telling it to gain sympathy or sainthood. I never once got the impression that she wanted me to enshrine her in public memory because of what she'd been through. I left her that day with the feeling that this woman knew what it was to surrender, not only a husband but also her right to sympathy.

Surrender. Where does it lead us?

It leads us right back to the position Jesus took one day when his disciples came into the room with dusty feet. Jesus grabbed a towel, knelt, and set about to wash their feet. It was surrender in its highest form. For when Jesus grabbed that towel, he was willingly placing himself at the feet of another. There to serve them. And is it any wonder he did it? For he said it himself: "Even the Son of Man did not come to be served, but to serve, and to give his life as a ransom for many" (Mark 10:45).

For every Christian who takes God at his Word, there is no way around it.

We are called to surrender.

And in our surrender we will find his peace.

It is a message we need to hear today, at a time when many of us are trying so frantically to hang on to our rights.

For Thought, Journaling, or Discussion:

1. Do you agree or disagree with this statement: "The notion of surrender has fallen on hard times among women today." Why?
2. What do you think is the most misunderstood thing about the notion of surrender?
3. Does surrender mean we always have to give in?
4. What, from your perspective, is a balanced view of surrender?
5. How would you describe God's view of surrender? Why do you think he makes a point of it in Scripture?
6. What are some images Scripture uses in speaking about surrender?
7. What are some examples from Scripture of people who surrendered? What were the results of their surrender?
8. Why do we find surrender so hard?
9. What are some ways you have found that make surrender work?
10. What results of surrender have you experienced?

NINE

....

*In the end, I think this is what women
truly desire: to know God and to stand tall
in their faith, strong at the core,
tender in heart.*

....

NINE

Empty on
the Inside?

Spiritual Discipline

One thing you can say for certain about many women these days: We *are* disciplined. We whip our schedules into shape, impose order in our work space, and condition our bodies without mercy. It seems we are forever bringing some part of our person, day, or home into line. For most of us, we *have* to apply ourselves to disciplined living or we would never achieve our goals.

But I have observed something interesting about the self-discipline of many women today. We do not apply to our faith the same rigor we bring to the rest of living. Perhaps we have to work so hard at life we have gotten lazy at developing spiritually. Yet a faith that is not cultivated (worked at as a farmer works the field—hoeing, raking, plowing, tilling) will never yield a harvest. We will have little faith substance to pass along to the next generation.

Strange, isn't it? In this day when many women know the secret of disciplined living, we've gotten to the place where discipline often has nothing to do with our faith, only with our bodies and our schedules and our parenting. *Give me a strong faith, yes, but don't put me through the rigors of having to grow it.*

On the other hand, maybe some of us want faith to come easy, just like we want everything else to come easy. We simply don't want to have to work hard. Period. At life. At our faith. At anything. And yes, there is a mindset among us that says: *Women today deserve a break. They have worked so hard for so long. Now is the time to just sit back and take it easy.* So we sit back and take it easy. Our faith is never disciplined because other areas of our life are not disciplined.

There is a third possibility as to why we don't work hard at faith discipline anymore. Maybe strong faith isn't even all that important to us these days. Everything else is. Maybe strong faith has become last seat in the orchestra, as far down in rank as it can go. We have faith, but why put ourselves through the rigors of growing it strong? After all, we can slide by. A form of godliness is easy to imitate. All we have to do is act a certain way.

I have heard it said, "Women today have lost their way."

It seems to me that whoever first uttered that was right. When we have lost spiritual disciplines (like prayer and Bible study), we *have* lost our way. "Your word is a lamp to my feet and a light for my path" (Psalm 119:105). Spiritual disciplines are the chart and compass of the soul, ever pointing us in right directions. Ever guiding us to right responses, right words, right actions. Without spiritual disciplines, we become soft on the inside. We are at the mercy of ourselves. And that is a very scary place to be.

Without spiritual disciplines, sooner or later our own vulnerability will do us in. We will have no weapons with which to fight our own unruly nature. Without prayer, faith, and the Word of God, the apostle Paul says we will have no strength, courage, or power to stand firm against the enemy. (See Ephesians 6:10–19.)

I remember a day when women worked hard at the things that made for strong faith—things like prayer and Bible study. There was a time and place when faith was all women had— their faith and hard work. So even as women worked hard, they prayed hard, studied their Bible hard, worshiped and served God with all their heart. Theirs was a fervent faith. And in the end, they had spiritual legacies of sizable proportions to hand down to the next generation.

They were women who pushed themselves to the limits for the sake of the kingdom. Nothing was too great a sacrifice, nothing too much an effort or inconvenience, if it meant they were getting to know God better and serving his kingdom in some way or other.

I remember such women.

———

I remember Anna.

She was for many years my Sunday school teacher. Our Sunday school class sat in three rows. Girls in front. Boys in back. We sat on old auditorium-type chairs. Four chairs in each row. (The chairs had been salvaged from an old school and given to Daddy for Sunday school rooms in the little church he was building down where the road curved between Miles Jackson's pasture and the woods.)

Our class met in a tiny cubicle of a room barely big enough for the twelve auditorium seats, Anna's wooden folding chair at the front, and a small gas heater that kept us warm on blustery winter days when the temperature got down to fifty.

One wall of the room boasted a chalkboard and the attendance chart, the other two walls a window each—so we could pay attention to the birds and trees and clouds should the lesson get boring. The fourth wall folded open to the primary classroom when we needed more space (like during Vacation Bible School and the Sunday school Christmas pageant).

The accommodations weren't spacious or even warm and inviting, but Anna was there, sitting on her hard wooden folding chair every Sunday for as long as Daddy was the pastor of that little country church—and even after we'd moved on. She taught me the Bible (even when I didn't really want to learn the Bible). Most of all, she gave me an appetite for studying the Word. (The appetite came long after the class with Anna ended.) I think Anna sat down to her big square pine kitchen table most every night of the week, after her supper dishes were cleared away, and studied her Sunday school lesson. (I dropped by her house often enough to see her doing it.)

And Anna prayed. Not just for herself. She prayed for China.

Every month, on the first Thursday afternoon, my mother and I would go to Anna's house. If the weather was nice (and it usually was), we'd sit on the big front porch rockers. On cooler days, we sat in front of the fireplace, surrounded by knotty pine walls and wonderful baskets of plants and flowers. (Anna could grow anything.) We went to Anna's house on this particular occasion each month solely to pray for the church in China.

I wasn't a seasoned veteran of prayer. I was a junior-higher more at home gathering eggs in the chicken house with Charlie (Anna's son) than I was praying. But I prayed with my mother and Anna anyhow. Anna had specific prayer requests written out for each of us on little pieces of paper. Before we prayed, she read us stories about Christian leaders in China and gave us all sorts of information about the country and the people and missionaries who worked there.

The stories captured my attention the most. I took home books Anna had sent away for and pulled out books my mother had collected over the years. Books about mission work. Books about China. I read them all. The world was suddenly much bigger than my little stand of pine trees and the grocery store/gas station/post office that stood at the bend in the road, marking the focal point of our community.

I learned about China. (To this day, a section of my library has books about the early days of mission work in China.) But most of all, I learned to pray. Not just for myself and for the people in my family and my church. I learned, as a junior-higher, to pray for the world. Not because I was a great spiritual giant, but because Mother and Anna included me. They were both women of prayer. And I suppose they wanted me to grow up to be a woman of prayer.

They taught me well. Even today, when my prayer life sadly limps along—and prayer time keeps getting buried under all those items of a more urgent, tangible nature—still, Anna and Mother taught me well. For I have the memory, strongly etched, of two women sitting on front-porch rockers in the woods of southern Alabama, praying for China—a continent and a half away. They were women greatly involved in the ministry of our little mission church, women with families to care for, large gardens to tend, farm chores to do, without gadgets of modern convenience to ease the load. And still they met every month just to pray for China.

I didn't understand the concept of "spiritual discipline" back then. But now I do. And I've decided it was what made women like Anna and my mother such remarkably strong women. They went to a lot of trouble for things that strengthened their faith. They knew what prayer could do for them. What it could do for China. (And we thought it was somewhere around the 1970s that women began to influence the world.) They (Anna and my mother) were innocent enough to believe prayer really worked. And they were focused enough to simply sit down and pray.

Most remarkable, not only did Anna and my mother nurture themselves in spiritual disciplines, they also nurtured their children in such disciplines. I took prayer so seriously in college that I got up early and locked myself in the broom closet at the end of the hall just to have a quiet time and a place to pray. Between my mother and Anna, they have raised two pastors, a minister's wife, a foreign missionary, and a Christian educator. All nine of their children are active in the work of the church.

While a woman's spiritual discipline does not guarantee anything for her children, it does guarantee that hers will be a stronger faith. And when hers is a strong faith, it is more likely that her children will understand the concept and latch on to it for themselves.

I remember women who prayed.

I remember women who read their Bibles as though it was as important as breakfast, lunch, or dinner; as though Jesus really meant it when he said, "Man [woman] does not live on bread alone, but on every word that comes from the mouth of God" (Matthew 4:4).

I don't know how many Bibles my mother has worn out. But they are many. As a child, I was always thinking: *Mother needs a new Bible.* Not because she never got a new Bible, but because no matter how new her Bible was, it always looked like she'd been using it for a long, long time.

And no wonder. There was nothing in the house my mother used more than her Bible. Not just once a day but all throughout the day her Bible was never far away. She read it like she read the newspaper—to see what was new. And the amazing thing was whenever she opened her Bible, she always seemed to be finding something new. And she never hesitated to pass on what she'd read and tell us how it fit into her day.

Talking about the Bible was for my mother as natural as talking about the weather. Maybe it is why I never resented her talking to me about it. It all seemed so right. So sensible. So extremely practical. I grew up thinking the Bible actually had something to do with real life.

Not much has changed with my mother over the years. She is still reading her Bible the same way. Wearing it out. Wanting to tell someone what she's just discovered.

"Mind if I read you what I just came across this morning?"

Mother is addressing my twenty-two-year-old, who just graduated from college. She knows he is uncertain what his next step should be.

He does not mind, so she reads from her Bible: "He will

teach us his ways, so that we may walk in his paths" (Isaiah 2:3).

Mother seems to feel no need to preach on the text. She lets the words stand on their own. I can tell my son has heard what she has read. He is thinking.

"Good word," he responds.

Then he is on to the sports page of the morning newspaper and mother is up and about, helping to clear away the breakfast dishes.

The Bible is that way to my mother. As relevant to today as the morning news. She has been reading it or hearing it for nearly eighty years, and it still isn't old hat.

How does that happen? I ask myself.

How does the Bible stay as fresh as the morning news to someone who has been familiar with it for close to eighty years?

It is, I think, because my mother comes to the Bible expecting to find something. She comes hungry, looking for nourishment. She opens her Bible often because she knows food is waiting for her there.

I wonder what would happen if we really expected the Bible to feed us, to provide us with spiritual energy and keep our spiritual systems in balance just like the basic food groups do for our bodies. If we really believed the Bible contained everything we needed for life and godliness (2 Peter 1:3). Think about it.

For one thing, maybe we would end up *knowing* what the Bible says. We would know the facts: where Abraham came from, who Zechariah was, and why Jesus had to move from Nazareth to Capernaum.

And we would know what sin is. We would see the devastation sin has caused. Maybe we would see enough to convince us: *I have to keep close to God or this could happen to me.*

Interestingly enough, it is impossible to stay close to God without staying close to his Word. Forget God's Word and it is just a matter of time until sin calls the shots in our lives.

If we kept to the Word of God like fish keep to the water, we would know what to do with ourselves. We would have the direction we need—and not the "turn left here" type of direction. (God does not fill in all the blue lines on the map for us.) But we would see the bigger picture. We would see our lives from God's perspective, and we would know what we have to do to get to where we should be. We would not always get so hung up on the moment if we kept reading our Bibles. For the Bible is always pointing us to something beyond ourselves. Something (or Someone, really) much, much bigger.

If we filled our minds with thoughts and words from the Bible, we would have plenty to think about during the day. We would not have to let our brain drift to romantic fantasies because it has nowhere else to go. Nor would fear play so large a part in our lives, stringing along our mind as we imagine all sorts of tragedies that could happen to us or our families. Think of all the headaches and backaches and tension of the jaw we *might* avoid. We might even get to sleep more easily at night if we went to sleep with a Bible verse (especially a Psalm) going through our mind.

And I also wonder, what might happen if women prayed more today? I mean the old-fashioned, down-on-your-knees, flat-out-on-your-face type of praying. The kind of praying where you forget what time it is and what's for lunch and where you have to go next.

For one thing, when we are down-under discouraged, empty with no more to give, we might find prayer to be our pipeline back to joy.

"You will fill me with joy in your presence" (Psalm 16:11).
We might find that prayer is restorative.

"He restores my soul" (Psalm 23:3).

That prayer can keep us from giving in to temptation.

"Watch and pray so that you will not fall into temptation" (Matthew 26:41).

If we were women who really knew how to pray, we might find that sometimes prayer is not a time or a place or even words. Sometimes it's just groanings that cannot be uttered. Sometimes it's just brokenness before God—a brokenness we desperately need because it brings us to the end of our self-sufficient rope. We cry out, "God, be merciful to me a sinner." (It is exactly the place God wants us to be.)

Prayer might turn us to the Cross again—the Cross where our sins still stare us in the face, for like it or not, we did help pound those nails. Though we are forgiven, still the Cross reminds us we blew it once, and we are just as likely to blow it again. That thought alone is enough to keeping us praying for all we're worth.

If we really knew how to pray, we might find that prayer could be the safety rope that keeps us from falling. We might learn that the more successful we are, the more we need to pray. The more power we possess, the more loved and appreciated and applauded we are, the more we need to pray.

We might find that prayer keeps our ego in check. In prayer we stand exposed. We cannot come into the throne room and stand before the King of Kings without his seeing us—all of us. And it is there that we realize he is looking at us. There is no place to hide in his presence. We finally get around to admitting to God what he has known about us all along—but was waiting for us to say.

If there is one guarantee to spiritual discipline it is this: We will be strong enough women to see God's hand in everything. And we will continually be saying, "Amazing! What an amazing God he is!" Bible study and prayer will continually bring us to this conclusion.

Like Mary, we will see beyond ourselves to the greatness of God. Mary—the one who carried the Son of God in her womb. Mary had a lot on her mind. She could have been stoned to death for being pregnant without a marriage license. She stood to lose her reputation. She knew little about being a mother, even less about housing the Son of God. The prospects were overwhelming.

But greatest on Mary's mind was this: *What an awesome God I have!* So that when she rang the doorbell at her cousin Elizabeth's house up in the hill country, it wasn't long before she was filling the place with her praise.

"My soul glorifies the Lord and my spirit rejoices in God my Savior, for he has been mindful of the humble state of his servant. From now on all generations will call me blessed, for the Mighty One has done great things for me—holy is his name. His mercy extends to those who fear him, from generation to generation" (Luke 1:46–50).

And Hannah.

Hannah wanted a son more than anything. She pleaded with God for a son. And God eventually gave her the son of her heart.

So what did she do? Run through the neighborhood showing him off? Sign him up for the best nursery school in town? No. She immediately turned Samuel, her son, over to God, to serve with Eli, the temple priest. And then, she started singing God's praises.

"My heart rejoices in the Lord; in the Lord my horn is lifted high. My mouth boasts over my enemies, for I delight in your deliverance. There is no one holy like the Lord; there is no one besides you; there is no Rock like our God. . . . For the foundations of the earth are the Lord's; upon them he has set the world. He will guard the feet of his saints" (1 Samuel 2:1–2, 8–9).

I read of such women and I am inspired to take the high road of spiritual discipline. For it is the high road of spiritual discipline that will keep me looking beyond myself and focusing on God.

The high road is not the easy road. Spiritual discipline is a slow, steady grind. The exercises of the soul are not noticed and applauded by others. The blood, sweat, and tears of it all are poured out behind closed doors—when no one is looking. No public citations or awards. Just quiet, solitary stretching the soul so there is more room for God. Always hungry for more of him. Always finding more of him. Getting up before dawn. Staying up long after bedtime. Letting other things go. Just so I can learn more of God.

"Blessed are those who hunger and thirst for righteousness, for THEY WILL BE FILLED" (Matthew 5:6, emphasis mine).

Where will the high road of spiritual discipline lead?

To God himself. And then back to authentic Christian living.

And in our authenticity, we will become not only women of action but women of character.

We will be honest through and through, not afraid that someday someone will peer into our soul and find a wasteland. When we tend the spirit, the garden within flourishes.

If we take the high road of spiritual discipline we will be granite-rock firm and solid. We will not be caught up with every wind that blows. For at our core will be the bedrock convictions for which we would die. We will know what we believe and why. We will be women of gracious conviction, standing tall against whatever it is that batters us on the outside.

For in the end, I think it is what we truly desire.

To know God and to stand tall in our faith, strong at the core, tender in heart.

To be kept "from falling and [to be presented] before his glorious presence without fault and with great joy" (Jude 24).

It is where the high road of spiritual discipline leads. It is where devoting ourselves to serious Bible study and prayer can eventually take us.

May God grant it, above all else, for women everywhere. For herein we will come to full maturity and strength.

For Thought, Journaling, or Discussion:

1. How would you define the word "discipline"?
2. What does the phrase "discipline of the faith" mean to you?
3. How does our culture work against the concept of this discipline?
4. Why do we need to work at our faith development if we don't have to work for our salvation? What is the difference?
5. What kinds of things cause you to get lazy in your faith?
6. How would you suggest that a woman go about disciplining her faith?
7. What has someone done for you or said to you that has helped you in your discipline of faith?
8. What does a disciplined faith look like?
9. Read Ephesians 6:10–19. How do the images Paul uses apply to the disciplining of one's faith?
10. After reading the above passage, what steps do you need to take to strengthen your faith?

TEN

....

*The sooner we rid ourselves of the notion
that women are a persecuted lot, the
sooner we can come to hope. And even if
abuse and exploitation and injustice have
been part of our past, there is still hope.*

....

Where Has Tomorrow Gone?

Hope

Not long ago I stood with a group of women and sang, "We are sisters on a journey. We are pilgrims on the road. . . ." It is a fitting image for women today as long as we don't focus so much on the journey yet to be taken that we forget the journey we *have* taken.

We've come a long way, baby. Yes.

But not far enough.

We've got a long way to go, baby.

That seems to have become our theme: *so far to go.*

And what is wrong with that theme?

Nothing. Except it focuses attention on progress not made rather than progress made. It casts our glance forward with a certain despair over the distance yet to go rather than backward with thanksgiving for the miles we *have* covered. It fills us with lament rather than with song. Sadder still, it causes us to be so busy looking back in disappointment that we never get around to seeing tomorrow with its good yet to come.

Maybe we have dwelt too long on what is not going right for women. Maybe we have pointed out too often how bleak the situation is. Maybe we've actually started to believe it. Maybe it is why we aren't very hopeful anymore.

True, now and then we hear or notice good things happening for women today. But we pay more attention to what is *not* happening. To how slowly we've been able to come into our own. How round about and up and down and hither and yon we've had to go to come into our own. How wrong things still are. How wrong. How wrong. How wrong.

It's all we seem to hear.

It's all we seem to think about. Or talk about.

What ever happened to the good old "Whatever is true, whatever is noble, whatever is right . . . whatever is admirable—if anything is excellent or praiseworthy—think about such things"? (Philippians 4:8). Think, talk, dwell on the good.

We tend not to do that today.

We have become a negative lot.

No wonder we are losing our grip on hope.

I wonder if we may not be losing our grip on hope because of how we view ourselves—as a persecuted group; and also because of how we view men—with a great deal of cynicism.

It seems to me, women today are losing their ability to

trust. We once trusted. Women once believed the world was basically a friendly place. People (men, to be specific) could be trusted. For the most part they cared about us. Respected us. They were generally kind, helpful, and considerate. (With numerous exceptions factored in, of course.) For the most part, we felt men would give us a fair deal. (The interesting thing is this: If we expect men to be basically kind and caring, oftentimes THAT IS EXACTLY HOW THEY WILL TREAT US. Treat them with distrust and we will get distrust in return.) Back then, that was more or less our point of view. We were not nearly so pessimistic about men and about life in general.

Oh, but we were young and idealistic when we believed all that. A few years experience and that view soured real quick.

Once upon a time, we were not so distrustful. We chose a brighter outlook—to still be hopeful about our future and the future of women everywhere.

We not only trusted men more, we still had tomorrow to look forward to. We were confident. The sun would shine. We would find fulfillment in our work—whatever that work happened to be.

Not that we thought things would always be easy for us. (We knew better.) But we were hopeful and confident enough about tomorrow to believe we would be able to handle whatever life brought us. God would still be good. Life would be an adventure. And we would be strong.

But somewhere along the line, our optimism began to fade. Our cynicism toward men became our cynicism toward many things. Toward relationships in general. Toward our government. Toward other Christians. Toward the church. Toward leadership of any kind. Today, we live on the dark side of distrust.

And what we do not trust, we also fear. In particular, we

fear where tomorrow will take us. If yesterday has not been that kind to us or delivered what it promised, how can we trust tomorrow? In our minds, tomorrow is at least as likely as today to be filled with bad news. So most of the time we would rather not even think about tomorrow. We would rather simply live for today. (There is plenty in today to keep us preoccupied or miserable, as the case may be.) And if ever we do get around to cracking the door on tomorrow, it is more out of fear or worry or dread than out of anticipation.

Such is the way of hopelessness.

Such is the road to despair.

––––––

But take the road to hope, and you have an entirely different perspective on life, on men.

For one, you have a *new* perspective.

Things are not where I'd like them to be. I am not where I'd like to be. Others are not where I'd like them to be. We are—all of us together—bungling along as best we can, helped out by an infinitely loving and patient heavenly Father who has designs on our future.

God has designs on our future.

It is a hopeful thought. It keeps us from fearing the future.

God has designed our future, and he has designed us for the future. He has given us something to do in the future that no one else can do. "And who knows but that you have come to royal position for such a time as this?" (Esther 4:14)

God has our blueprint rolled out on his desk before him. Our future is not a nebulous thought out there somewhere in his mind. It is a planned future.

" 'For I know the plans I have for you,' declares the Lord, 'plans to prosper you and not to harm you, plans to give you hope and a future' " (Jeremiah 29:11).

Start believing these words, and hopelessness will eventually have to exit by the back door.

What we must start believing is this: God is not out to do us in. Usually, men are not out to do us in either. (The sooner we rid ourselves of the notion that we are a persecuted lot, the sooner we can come to hope.) And even if abuse and exploitation and injustice have been part of our past, there is still hope.

God has not done me in, even if a man has. Tomorrow holds good things.

Hope has a greater luster about it when it has grown in the dark. Trusting God as we work through abuse and exploitation is more of a reach on our part. It calls for a greater determination to lay hold of hope. And where there is determination on our part, there are the resources on God's part. "May the God of hope fill you with all joy and peace as you trust in him, so that you may overflow with *hope* by the power of the Holy Spirit" (Romans 13:13).

God plans to give us a future and a hope. The only thing that can change his plan is for us to deny him the privilege.

———

Women of hope do not cower at the thought of tomorrow. Rather, they say, *I will trust God for tomorrow and I will not be afraid.*

And then they hang on to hope with everything in them. They simply refuse to give up. Ever. They do not give up on God. They do not give up on other people. They do not give up on themselves.

"We who have fled to take hold of the hope offered to us may be greatly encouraged" (Hebrews 6:18).

Hope does that—it encourages. It does something else for

us—it settles us down, calms our free-for-all, our bouncing all over the place. It causes us to lock into commitment.

I believe in tomorrow, therefore I will commit myself to it.

Hope keeps us in place.

"We have this *hope* as an anchor for the soul, firm and secure" (Hebrews 6:19).

Hope is the great stabilizer. With hope, we stay grounded in God and connected to the people to whom we've committed ourselves. Love and hope are intricately linked.

"Love . . . always hopes" (1 Corinthians 13:6–7).

Sometimes hope is all we have going for us—in our marriage, for example. Hope means we intend to hang on.

This marriage may not be all it should be, but today I will take one step toward making it what God wants it to be. Good things may not have happened in the past. But good things can be ahead for my marriage. I will hang on.

If every married person said this every day of their lives, divorce courts would go out of business. And we would live with a new sense of mission when it comes to making our marriages work.

————

Women of hope count on the notion that other people eventually come around. Women of hope know God for his amazing ability to rotate people 360 degrees.

God can change people. Scripture is full of the records. Transformation is what the power of the Gospel is all about.

Well, I sure hope God changes this person fast before he drives me to a nervous breakdown.

That is not hope. It is wishful thinking. And wishful thinking usually contains great amounts of selfishness. We want God to change another person so things will be easier for us.

But that is not how God does it. He does not change people so we can be more optimistic about our future. He changes another for that person's sake, not for ours.

Women of hope remain optimistic, despite doubtful signs. They remain hopeful for the other person's good. They don't merely "hope for the best." (That has a sigh and a tinge of doubt attached to it.) But they hold to their conviction that God is redeeming all things in his own time and in his own way. And should the other person choose NOT to let God change them, women of hope still believe "all things are possible." They never give up on this fundamental truth.

Hope is really about tomorrow. It looks on the bright side of tomorrow, even when it is on the dark side of today.

It sees through the murk enough to say, *Things are pretty bleak right at the moment, but I will look forward to something in the future, even if I have to plan something for myself.*

Sometimes planning something we've always wanted to do can be the most practical way to help ourselves along toward hope. Sometimes having something to look forward to can actually bring us back to life.

My mother and I had always planned to take a trip to England. Someday. We talked about it casually over the years. Mother had even saved her money for it. But one day, that plan took on life-saving proportions.

It is day number five since my mother has gone on the respirator. She lies, eyes closed, small and almost indistinguishable among the tangle of tubes and wires. It is not a time for despair, but I am deep in its clutches. No sign of life in this intensive care unit cubicle this morning except for the Darth Vader-like sounds coming from the respirator. No sign of life in my mother. No sign of hope in me.

But it is just like hope never to give up. Sometimes hope pushes its way even through the darkest of dark.

"Talk to your mother," the nurse says. "Talk about something she can look forward to. We *have* to get her off this respirator."

England.

It is the only thought I can muster.

My mother has been looking forward to our taking a trip to England someday.

I lean over Mother's bed and I say, "Mother. You have to hurry and get well so we can go to England."

At the word "England," my mother opens her eyes. She looks at me and SHE WINKS.

In that wink I hear these words: *I will get well. I will take that trip to England with my daughter.*

I see determination reborn in that wink, hope revived.

I go home that night and start planning the trip.

It is the rebirth of hope, yes. But it is also the beginning of that long and treacherous year of recovery. All during those icy winter months, Mother and I look forward to England. We look forward to it so much we can actually see ourselves boarding the plane for London, driving the countryside, strolling the gardens. Some days, it feels as though we are taking one step forward toward England, five steps backward toward physical relapse. But always, the picture of England remains in our thoughts—firmly fixed, clearly visible.

Finally, Mother is well and the time comes: We board the plane for England. During the next ten days, we drive the countryside, stroll the gardens, thinking often about the part hope played in Mother's journey back to health.

Something good is coming.

The thought spurred us on.

And it is that precise thought women today need to reclaim.

Good things *have* happened. And good things *will* happen. We will trust and not be dismayed. We will trust and not be afraid.

————————

And here is the lesson from my mother's story: *When we give ourselves something to look forward to, no matter how great or small the event, we are giving ourselves the gift of hope. And where there's hope built into tomorrow, there are all kinds of possibilities for overcoming whatever obstacle we face today.*

Hang on to hope and tomorrow will stretch before you, full of images of good things to come. Even this life, filled though it is with disappointment, can also be filled with the thought: *Good things are coming. Even in the midst of the bad, good things are coming.*

For the Christian woman, good things are coming because God is coming.

It is the ultimate hope—this anticipation that rings through the words of the apostle Paul when he writes about "the blessed hope—the glorious appearing of our great God and Savior, Jesus Christ" (Titus 2:13).

It is the hope David must have felt when he sang, "Surely goodness and love will follow me all the days of my life, and I will dwell in the house of the Lord forever" (Psalm 23).

Hope is what faith is all about—being 100 percent confident that good things are coming because God is coming.

"Now faith is being sure of what we hope for" (Hebrews 11:1).

Hope lives with this anticipation: We will see God.

Hope knows that on that day when we see God, we will be as we were meant to be—male and female, in perfect harmony. We will stand together and sing the victor's song. And the song we sing will be this:

"Worthy is the Lamb, who was slain, to receive power and wealth and wisdom and strength and honor and glory and praise!" (Revelation 5:12).

Finally, women's issues will be forever laid to rest. Our focus will be all on God.

Then, we will truly be able to say:

By God's grace, we (all of us, men and women alike) *have* come a long way.

Then the celebration will begin. And when the first thousand years are up, the party will only have started.

———

Meanwhile, we have every reason to be women of hope.

Every reason to hold tenaciously to those qualities that made our mothers and grandmothers strong.

Every reason to lift our heads and say with thanksgiving: *We're not there yet. But praise the Lord, we are well on the road.*

And may our journey continue with great love, humility, and understanding.

That in the end we may say:

By God's grace, yes, we have come a long, long way.

For Thought, Journaling, or Discussion:

1. What are some examples from Scripture of people who could not see the future because they were so caught up in the despair of the moment?
2. Did they ever regain hope? If so, how?
3. What do these examples say to you about despair? What do they say to you about hope?
4. Trace the word "hope" through Scripture. What conclusions do you come to about hope?
5. How might these conclusions apply to the male/female issues of today?
6. How would you attempt to guide a disillusioned woman back toward hope?
7. How have you regained hope during a time of disappointment and hurt?
8. How can hopeful living make a difference?
9. What is the difference between hope and naiveté? Between hope and optimism?
10. What is the link between our future hope and our hope for today?